D1147276

ETHICS IN
NURSING PRACTICE

ETHICS IN NURSING PRACTICE

Graham Rumbold

BA, SRN, NDN, CHNT, DNT, RNT
Senior Lecturer in District Nursing
Nene College, Northampton

Baillière Tindall London Philadelphia
Toronto Sydney Tokyo

Baillière Tindall 24–28 Oval Road
W.B. Saunders London NW1 7DX.

The Curtis Center
Independence Square West
Philadelphia, PA 19106-3399, USA.

1 Goldthorne Avenue
Toronto, Ontario M8Z 5T9, Canada

Harcourt Brace Jovanovich Group (Australia)
PTY Ltd., 32–35 Smidmore Street, Marrickville,
NSW 2204, Australia.

Harcourt Brace Jovanovich (Japan) inc.
Ichibancho Central Building, 22-1 Ichibancho
Chiyoda-ku, Tokyo 102, Japan.

First published 1986
Reprinted 1989

Typeset by Inforum Ltd, Portsmouth
Printed in Great Britain by The Alden Press, Oxford

British Library Cataloguing in Publication Data

Rumbold, Graham
  Ethics in nursing practice.
  1. Nursing ethics
  I. Title
  174′.2   RT85

ISBN 0-7020-1155-X

Printed in Great Britain by
The Alden Press, Oxford

CONTENTS

Foreword, vii

Preface, ix

Acknowledgements, xi

1 What is Right? 1

2 Cultural Influences on Ethical Decision Making, 13

3 Sanctity of Life versus Quality of Life, 27

4 For the Good of Whom? 37

5 Duties, Rights, Responsibilities, 48

6 Euthanasia, 61

7 The Unborn Child, 72

8 Hospitals Should Do the Patient No Harm, 87

9 Confidentiality, 101

10 To Tell or Not to Tell, 111

11 The Nurse–Doctor Relationship, 122

12 The Rights of the Nurse, 139

Index, 153

FOREWORD

The publication of this book – *Ethics in Nursing Practice* – is most timely, coming at a period when doctors, nurses and other members of the health professions are beset with ethical dilemmas. Some of these have been with us over the years, and others have arisen or become more complex due to medical and scientific advances.

The pressures are felt most keenly by the clinical nurse caring for the patient in hospital or the home. This book is aimed at the senior student nurse and the qualified nurse, making it particularly relevant for the ward or district nursing sister and members of their nursing teams, nurses taking post-basic training, and those working in specialized units. At the same time, it will be invaluable for the nurse teacher and the nurse manager, each with their separate responsibilities for guiding both the qualified and the student nurse.

Ethics is a complex subject, and the nurse using this book should not expect to find easy reading. The book falls into two sections, the first discussing some of the major value systems affecting moral decision making, the second analysing specific issues relevant to nursing and health care based on ethical theories discussed in the first section. The principles are set out in a readable manner and the examples are credible and meaningful to the nurse. If the aim of nurse education is to prepare a safe beginning practitioner with an enquiring mind, here is a book which guides the nurse through the argument and leaves him/her with the decision making.

The author is uniquely placed to write this book. He is an experienced clinical nurse whose main field of practice has been as a district nurse, and he has been engaged in teaching district nurses for many years. During this latter period he undertook theological training on a part-time basis and was ordained priest in the Church of England in 1979. For the last five years he has combined his post as Senior Lecturer in District Nursing with that of Chaplain to Cynthia Spencer House, the continuing care unit in Northampton. He is, therefore, in day-to-day contact with nurses and patients in his pastoral work, and with his post-registration students, as can be seen by his frequent references to their experiences and attitudes.

This is an obvious book for every library in a school of nursing and hopefully will find a place in libraries used by all members of the health professions. It is also a book for the private bookshelf of every nurse, both to read in order to acquire a sound knowledge of value systems and ethical issues, and to turn to in times of particular questions and difficulties.

November 1985   *Sheila Quinn CBE*

PREFACE

The impetus to write this book comes after many years in nursing, both in practice and in teaching, and as the outcome of teaching ethics to nurses. One of the main difficulties I have faced in teaching ethics has been the lack of textbooks written specifically from a nursing standpoint. There are numerous medical texts but only a few nursing texts and those are for the most part written within the context of nursing in America. Although the book is written by a nurse with nurses in mind it is hoped that other health care professionals will find in it much of relevance. The thoughts contained in the book are in part my own, partly those of other writers, and to some considerable extent drawn from discussions I have had with nurses, patients and families, both as a nurse and as a hospital chaplain.

Nurses and others involved in the delivery of health care frequently find themselves in the position of making decisions which are not solely of a clinical or nursing nature, but of a moral or ethical nature. On occasions a person might make a decision which on the face of it is essentially a clinical one, and yet his decision will be influenced, perhaps unconsciously, by his ethical beliefs and values. The nurse therefore needs to examine her own beliefs and the bases on which she makes decisions.

The purpose of this book is two-fold: firstly to give an introduction to ethical theories in order to provide the nurse with a framework within which to make decisions and an understanding of how others might arrive at their decisions, and secondly to explore some of the main areas of debate within health care delivery. The book is divided into two parts. Chapters 1–5 discuss some of the major philosophical and cultural approaches to ethics and morals, and relates as much as possible general theories to nursing and health care situations. In Chapters 6–12 the approach is to take specific issues or areas of concern and examine some of the ethical arguments surrounding them.

This book does not set out to provide answers or a blueprint for action, but to provide the nurse with a theoretical basis on which to formulate her* own answers. Hopefully too the reader will be helped to further develop skills of philosophical thinking and reasoning which enable one to work through problems more quickly and efficiently.

Not everyone faced with a question of a moral or ethical nature will arrive at the same answer. One's answer will depend to a large extent on one's cultural and religious background. It is important that the nurse has an understanding, not only of those factors which affect her own decision making, but those factors which influence the decisions of others.

As medical technology advances, so the range of ethical issues increases. Nurses today face situations unknown to their predecessors of 100 or even 50 years ago. The 'right' responses to these situations are not to be found specifically in the traditional sources of ethical teaching, such as the Bible, the Koran or the Talmud, for the very good reason that they are situations of which the great moral teachers of the past could not possibly conceive. Philosophy and ethics are no more static than science and medicine. Philosophical enquiry frequently raises new questions and new theories about problems both old and new. To find answers to today's problems we have not only to look back to answers of yesterday but also to examine them in the light of today's knowledge and experience.

No individual can opt out of making moral decisions, and because of the rapidly changing world in which we live no one can rely on another's thinking in making those decisions. Moral decisions are by nature personal. At the end of the day we have to be able to square our consciences. Nevertheless, to start with a blank sheet is difficult and unnecessary. The purpose of books such as this one is to help people come to their own decisions.

Graham Rumbold

---

* Purely for the sake of ease and convenience throughout this book the nurse is generally referred to as being female and the patient and doctor as male.

ACKNOWLEDGEMENTS

Many people have contributed to the preparation of this book. I am particularly grateful to students, both past and present, who have provided much of the background discussion and the case studies. I must express my sincere thanks to Rosemary Morris, Nursing Editor for Baillière Tindall, without whose patient encouragement and gentle cajoling the rather loose ideas in my head would never have been formed into the book now in your hand. I also thank the reviewers for their helpful advice and suggestions which, as much as possible, have been woven into the text.

Finally I must thank Mrs Vardy for typing the manuscript so speedily and accurately.

1

WHAT IS RIGHT?

At its most basic the study of ethics is concerned with the meaning of such words as *right, wrong, good, bad, ought, duty.* It is concerned with the basis on which people, individually or collectively, decide that certain actions are right or wrong, and whether one ought to do something or has a right to something. This chapter will begin to discuss what determines whether particular actions are right and if some actions are always right whatever the circumstances in which they occur.

Virginia Henderson (1977) gives as one of her components of basic nursing care 'helping the patient practise his religion or conform to his concept of right and wrong'. At one time it was fairly safe to assume that a nurse working in the Western world would share the same religious faith, i.e. Christian, and the same concept of right and wrong as at least the majority of her patients. This certainly cannot be said of the second half of the 20th century. It is no longer the case that all nurses will share the same set of religious or moral values, and nor will their patients. Each individual's set of values will be the result of a multitude of factors, e.g. family mores, religious, cultural and educational background, and peer group influences. Nurses as a professional group are divided in their opinions with regard to issues such as abortion, euthanasia and medical research. Views among nurses will range from those who would argue that abortion, for example, is wrong whatever the circumstances, through those who would say it is permissible in certain circumstances, to those who believe that every woman should have the right to have her pregnancy terminated on demand.

The end justifies the means

Contained within most moral codes, and certainly those of the major world religions, is the idea that to take human life, at least in most circumstances, is wrong. Equally it is a fairly generally held belief that to save life is right. It is however only a minority view that the taking of human life is wrong in all circumstances. Throughout

1

man's history killing has been justified in certain situations, e.g. in war, as a punishment, or as an act of mercy. Therefore, it would seem that it is not so much the act of killing itself that is held to be wrong as the reason for doing it. To kill an enemy during time of war is held to be justifiable because it is done not out of malice but for some good, the good being the protection of the State, the preservation of freedom, and the protection of one's fellow countrymen. Similarly, the killing of criminals, in particular murderers, has been justified on the grounds that society thereby rids itself of evil and prevents the criminal from causing further harm to society or individuals within society. Mercy killing can be justified on the grounds that it prevents the recipient from suffering further pain. This latter issue is far more complex and the subject of euthanasia will be discussed fully in Chapter 6.

What lies behind all these arguments is the idea that the end justifies the means. If the end result is a good one, for example the protection of the State, then the means by which that end is achieved is also, if not good, at least justifiable and permissible. The implications of an ends-justifies-the-means philosophy are far-reaching, and not least within the bounds of nursing and medical practice. Such a philosophy could, for example, justify the experimental use of drugs on patients, which might be harmful to the individuals concerned, on the grounds that the ultimate end of such experiments was good, namely to produce a cure for a particular disease and so prevent much suffering.

In Nazi Germany, doctors carried out a vast range of experiments on the inmates of concentration camps. Cancer was introduced into subjects and the progress of their agonizing deaths recorded. Others were stood naked for many hours in below-freezing temperatures; they were then warmed up to see at what points they showed vital life signs. Many died in the process and the remainder were usually killed afterwards. One of the Nazi scientists involved in these freezing experiments went to the United States after the war where he was to pioneer the development of American space medicine (Meltzer 1975).

Suppose that the purpose of the first of these experiments was to discover a cure for cancer, and suppose further that a cure was in fact discovered as a direct result of them: Would the experiments have been justified? The outcome would indeed have been of immense good; the suffering of many thousands in future generations would have been prevented. Suppose too, that as a direct result of the freezing experiments the scientist responsible was able to advance the development of space medicine beyond all reasonable expectations: Would those experiments be justified? The answer of most people to these questions would probably be 'no'. Many would say that such acts were wrong in themselves regardless of the end.

The examples discussed so far are of a dramatic nature and do not form part of most people's everyday experiences. Let us now apply these arguments to less dramatic situations. Ask yourself whether you agree or disagree with the following statements:

1 To tell the truth is right.
2 One should tell the truth on all occasions.
3 There are occasions when to tell a lie is justified.

I cannot know your response to these statements, but I suspect that most readers would agree with the first statement, but that there would be debate about the other two.

Is it right or wrong to admire a friend's hat even if one thinks it terrible? It is something most of us have done at one time or another. In this case to tell the truth would cause the friend distress, may lead to an argument or further exchange of home truths. The end result of telling a lie is the happiness of the friend. No harm is done – or is it? The friend would no doubt continue to wear the hat and might make herself a laughing stock. Generally in such circumstances we couch our comments in words and phrases which while not reflecting our true feelings are not blatant untruths. We tend to call such statements 'white lies' and as such they are a generally accepted part of social interaction.

In the United Kingdom, as in most countries, when a person enters the witness box in a court of law they are required to swear an oath to the effect that the evidence they will give will be truth, the whole truth and nothing but the truth. The very fact that in the special circumstance of a court of law one is required to take such an oath suggests that in normal day-to-day life people do not, nor are they expected to, tell the truth all the time.

Let us consider the following case. Susan and Jane are close friends. One day Susan tells Jane that she has been unfaithful to her husband, Bob. Susan asks Jane to tell no one, least of all Bob. What does Jane do? At this stage, having given Susan advice, perhaps suggesting that she ought to tell her husband, Jane is faced with a problem. Does she tell Bob or does she maintain silence? Her decision will depend on several factors: what she knows about Susan's and Bob's relationship, her own relationship with both

Susan and Bob, and her own views on the rightness or wrongness of adultery. Jane may decide at this stage to remain silent on the grounds that Susan's unfaithfulness was a one-off event, and that to tell Bob would lead to more harm than good.

What then if two weeks later Jane meets Bob, he tells her that he suspects Susan of being unfaithful, and asks Jane if Susan has said anything to her? The problem is now more acute. It could be argued that to lie, to say she knows nothing, is justified. Firstly, the information was given her in confidence and therefore to tell would be breaking that confidence and could have harmful effects in terms of a lost friendship. Secondly, by denying all knowledge Jane might put Bob's fears at rest and prevent the possible break-up of the marriage. If, on the other hand, Bob later finds out that Jane has lied, this could lead to a loss of his friendship and the other consequences which she had tried to alleviate.

To tell the truth could have harmful effects, but might equally have beneficial effects. By telling the truth Jane might be able to explain the circumstances in which the act of unfaithfulness occurred and help Bob come to terms with the situation and thus save the marriage. Alternatively, he might react violently, return home and attack Susan, or walk out on her.

The problem we face when making decisions of this kind is that we can only hazard guesses at the possible outcomes. However good our intentions we cannot predict or control the course of events. Proponents of an ends-justifies-the-means ethic would argue that if the intention is to effect a good end the means chosen is justified. Therefore if Jane lied to Bob in order to effect a good end then her action would be right, even if the end she tried to bring about did not occur. There is an inherent weakness in this line of argument. For a start it can be used to justify almost any kind of action, even those as extreme as the Nazi atrocities. We would do well to remember the old proverb: *The road to hell is paved with good intentions.* Secondly, we need to consider all the possible consequences of our actions.

If the deciding factor in judging whether an action is right or wrong is the intended consequences, then the criteria on which the decision is made are:
1 that the consequences are good or evil according to whether and how much they serve humane values; and
2 that the means to achieve those consequences are not so bad as to outweigh the goodness of the final outcome.
If the ultimate end is human happiness and well-being, but the

means to achieving that end in itself creates unhappiness and suffering, which outweigh the goodness of the final result, the end cannot justify the means. For the end to justify the means the end itself has to be good, and a morally *good* end can justify a *bad* means on the principle of proportionate good. As we shall see in later chapters, this line of argument is used to justify such acts as abortion, euthanasia and deceiving a patient about his or her diagnosis.

Principle of double effect

There would be few who on reading about the Nazi atrocities would not react with horror and say 'No, such acts cannot be justified however good the end.' Such acts are, it would seem, held by most to be essentially wrong in themselves. Some would go still further and take a more absolute or purist view with regard to various acts. The pacifist, for example, would take the view that killing whatever the circumstances is wrong, because the act itself is wrong and cannot therefore be justified. What then if the refusal to do one wrong act results not in good but in further wrong? What if a man's refusal to kill a terrorist results in his own death and those of his wife and family? The result of his non-action is bad, although his motives in not acting were essentially good. The decision not to act is a moral or ethical one and can therefore be judged as being right or wrong just as a decision to act. A person does not abdicate moral judgement by doing nothing.

In situations such as this we have an example of what is described as the principle of double effect. In a situation in which to act will have undesirable consequences, and not to act will also have undesirable consequences, we have to weigh up whether to undertake the act. If the man does nothing the effect will almost inevitably be the death of himself and family. If he acts and kills the terrorist, assuming he is successful, then this too will have undesirable effects – the death of another human being and feelings of guilt brought about by carrying out an act which he holds to be morally wrong. If he is unsuccessful in his attempt to kill the terrorist then in all probability the terrorist will kill him and his family. The end result will be the same as if he had done nothing.

In the earlier case discussed, Jane was faced with a similar dilemma – to tell or not to tell Bob of Susan's infidelity. The consequences of either course of action could be harmful. Jane's problem was, until confronted by Bob, considerably easier than that of the man faced with a terrorist. Jane at least had time to think, time to weigh up the consequences. Unfortunately, very often we do not have that luxury; the decision has to be made on the spot.

In making decisions of this kind there are four criteria which should be met, namely:

1 The act itself must be morally good, or at least neutral.
2 The purpose must be to achieve the good consequence, the bad consequence being only a side effect.
3 The good effect must not be achieved by way of the bad, but both must result from the same act.
4 The bad result must not be so serious as to outweigh the advantage of a good result.

If the man decides to kill the terrorist, then (1) and (4) might give rise to debate. The question arises as to whether the act of killing can ever be morally good or even neutral. It could be argued in this case that it was neutral, for it could be argued that a man has a duty to protect his wife and family, and therefore if he refused to do so would be morally negligent. With regard to the fourth criterion, the bad result – the death of a person – could be argued to outweigh the advantage of a good result – the protection of wife and children. The problem of course is not that clear-cut. For if the man chooses to avoid the bad result on the grounds that it outweighs the advantages of the good result, then the actual result will be bad – the death of several persons. His deciding not to act in order to avoid one bad result will have resulted in an even worse consequence.

There are many situations in medicine and nursing in which the doctor or nurse is faced with making decisions, and whichever decision is taken will have harmful consequences. Consider the situation in which a doctor is caring for a patient who is terminally ill and in severe pain. The doctor knows that the dosage of analgesia needed to relieve the pain is such that it will also hasten death. Death in such a case might be described as a side effect of the treatment. It is clearly the doctor's duty to try to relieve the patient's pain. Not to give analgesia in order to avoid death, which is inevitable anyway, and leave the patient in agony would not be ethically defensible. Of the four criteria only the fourth might be an area for debate in this situation. The side effect, death, might be considered to be so serious as to outweigh the advantages of a good result, pain relief. However, since death is inevitable, and will almost certainly be due to the disease, all that the doctor would be doing is making the process of dying easier and gentler for the patient. What it comes back to in the end is the consequence at which the act is aimed. The doctor is not aiming at the death of the patient, but at relief of his suffering.

Natural law

In most situations when faced with a moral dilemma people do not sit down and weigh up all the consequences. What in practice happens is that people act almost instinctively according to their own set of rules and values. Some people hold very firm views as to what constitutes right or wrong. Some, like the pacifist, would say that all that has to be considered is the rightness or wrongness of the act itself and not the circumstances in which it occurs, nor the consequences of the act. It has been argued that just as there are natural laws governing the physical universe, such as the laws of gravity, so there are natural moral laws. If there is a natural moral law which determines what is morally right in any given situation it is binding on everyone and would therefore be absolute.

In Western theological systems, for example, which are monotheistic, God is the ultimate test of morality. Any action would be judged as being right or wrong according to whether it adhered to God's law. The question is how can we know what is the divine law? Both Christianity and Judaism hold that the divine law has been revealed to man through his prophets and teachers, and, in the case of Christianity, through Christ. The account of God's revelation of his law are the scriptures. In addition, some Christian thinkers have argued that moral law can be discovered through the use of human reason.

It is not, however, only believers in these two religions who hold that there is a natural moral law. Indeed it is not necessary to believe in any divine source of moral law to believe that a universal moral framework exists. This is true of the Stoics and of present day secular natural law and natural rights theories. The United Nations' *Declaration of Human Rights*, for example, states that every human being has certain rights, such as the rights to justice, freedom and 'a standard of living adequate for the health and well-being of himself'. Whereas those whose base for determining natural law is a theological one rely largely on revelation as the source of knowledge, non-theological based thinking relies on reason, observation, or intuition as ways of determining what is the natural law.

Immanuel Kant[1] argued that reason, or *practical reason* as he called it, can discover that there are certain rules of behaviour, or maxims, which become a universal law of nature. He argued that the way of determining if a moral principle or rule existed was to ask what the effects would be if it were to be applied universally. If the overall effect was good then to behave in that way was right and in accordance with natural moral law. What would be the effect if everyone always told the truth? The effect would surely be one of universal good; therefore to tell the truth is a natural law. This is somewhat of a simplification of Kant's theory, but it does serve to illustrate how natural law can be arrived at through reason.

Others have held that the basis for moral judgement can be discovered by observation. According to this view, we are equipped with a moral capacity to sense what the laws of nature are. Roderick Firth (1952), for example, argues that morality is absolutist in the sense of being independent of the observer. An action is right if it would produce a feeling of approval in an ideal observer, such an observer being one who is impeccably sensitive, impartial, consistent and dispassionate, but otherwise normal. Firth, and others, do not claim that such a person exists but merely that if he or she did we would hold as right anything which met with his or her approval. Firth says that in his ideal observer he has given what might be construed as a partial description of God. However, a belief in God or some other infinite being is not an intrinsic part of this moral standpoint.

If such an ideal observer does not exist we cannot, others have argued, determine definitely what his or her feelings would be. We have to rely in the end on our own feelings or intuition. The intuitionist holds that moral truths may be known to be true by intuition, i.e. that they are if properly considered simply self-evident.

Whether natural law is discovered by revelation, reason, observation or intuition, those who hold that such a law does exist have a clear framework on which to base ethical decisions, and a set of clear and binding guidelines on which to make decisions. These guidelines could then be applied to all situations including nursing and medical ones. There would be no need for specific medical or nursing codes of ethics, for all one would need to do would be to refer to natural law.

If a patient reveals in confidence to a nurse or doctor that he intends to commit a murder, the question is should the nurse or doctor disclose this information. To do so will have the effect of preventing the patient from acting and save the life of the intended victim. In a situation such as this we should turn, not to any professional code of ethics, but to some framework which is more relevant to the problem at hand – to God's will or the natural law discovered by man's reason or through the moral senses. Thus the greater universal law that we should not take life and have a duty to save life would override any invented moral code which might hold that we should respect confidentiality or that the patient has a right to expect it.

While the concept of natural moral law has much to offer in terms of making ethical decisions more easy and clear-cut, it does have some weaknesses. We cannot be absolutely certain that we know what it is. This applies whether the basis is that of revelation, reason or observation. Throughout the centuries there has been argument about what has been revealed and how that revelation should be interpreted. Men have reasoned differently from society to society and from age to age. Since no ideal observer is thought to exist, this school of thought relies heavily on man's moral sense and the laws arrived at vary and are unreliable.

Probably the strongest argument against natural law theories is that acceptance of a universally binding rule removes the element of choice. Since I have the ability to reason and decide for myself what is right or wrong, to not use that reasoning ability would in itself be contrary to natural law.

Natural law is often invoked when discussing the question of contraception, for nowhere is natural law more assiduously applied than in the area of sexuality. Proponents of natural law say that God or nature intended sexual intercourse to result in pregnancy. To prevent the occurrence of pregnancy is to interfere with the natural course of events; it is to violate natural law and is therefore wrong. The question is: Do we have the right to control events? If it is wrong to control the natural physiological process of conception, then it must equally be wrong to attempt to control other natural courses of events. We attempt to control many events that occur in nature; we build dykes and sea walls to prevent flooding and we build irrigation canals to prevent the formation of deserts. Is it any more or less moral to protect lives and homes by building flood barriers to control the rush of flood waters into a city such as London than to use a sheath to prevent the rush of spermatozoa to the womb? There is certainly a degree of illogicality in a line of thought which allows the one, but disallows the other.

The question arises as to whether the only purpose of human sexual intercourse is procreation. It is a fact that within each 28-day menstrual cycle conception is only probable during five to six days. Yet a woman's desire for sexual intercourse extends beyond that limited time. Unlike many other animals, human beings desire, are capable of, and enjoy sexual intercourse at times when the woman is not fertile. Therefore it would seem that reproduction is only one purpose of sexual intercourse, and on the basis of time ratio relatively less important than pleasure. It is argued that another purpose of intercourse is an expression of love and affection; it is a means of communication. It is pleasurable because nature intended us to have intercourse for reasons other than the reproduction of the species.

Human beings are as they are as a result of the natural evolutionary process. That process has equipped us with the knowledge and ability to control our environment and our bodies. As a result we have a freedom of choice in being able, amongst other things, to control our reproductive environment. It can be argued that exercising that choice is to exhibit a higher level of morality than leaving reproduction to chance. Since human beings have evolved to this stage, and since evolution is a natural process, not to use those evolved capabilities and to behave as if the possibility of control was not there would be against natural law.

The fact that we have the ability to do something does not of course make the doing of it right. We have the ability to destroy ourselves with nuclear weapons but it would be extremely difficult to justify doing so. There is a difference between preventing conception by unnatural means, and destroying ourselves and the world in which we live. In the first instance we are merely controlling one natural process in order to allow another natural process to proceed unhindered. In the second instance we would not be controlling a natural process but totally destroying the whole course of nature and not even replacing it with anything else.

We have the ability to reason and to make rational decisions. To not use that ability, to act purely on the basis of a set of irrational rules, would be wrong. If using our ability to reason we conclude that contraception is wrong then that is a morally mature decision, but so too would be to conclude that it was right. Either conclusion could be said to be in line with natural law.

Summary

There is no easy answer to the question posed in the title of this chapter – *What is right?* Different people have put forward a variety of different ways of determining whether particular actions are right. One way of deciding is to consider the consequences; this I have called the *end-justifies-the-means-ethic*. This idea forms an essential part of what is generally known as *utilitarianism*. There are different types of utilitarianism of which possibly the most well known is that of Jeremy Bentham. Bentham and his disciple John Stuart Mill held that what determined whether an act was right or wrong was the extent to which it lead to human happiness. It is from them that we get the phrase *the greatest happiness for the greatest number*. As we have seen, there are limitations to a line of argument based on either known or intended outcomes, and particularly where the outcome is merely hoped for but not known for certain.

The idea of natural law, while providing a framework on which to base ethical decisions, does not always meet the needs of the situation nor is it always easily discernible. What does one do when faced with a situation which is not covered by any known natural law?

In the following chapters we will examine further some of the questions and ideas raised in this chapter. We shall look at the influence of major world religions and ideologies on ethical thinking and in particular what they have to say about natural or divine law. We shall return too to the idea that the end justifies the means and in particular consider whether the end aimed at should be the good of the community or society as a whole or the good of the individual. Other theories will be examined, such as duty-based and rights-based theories, and their contribution to determining what is right.

Notes

1 Immanuel Kant, 1724–1804, was born of devout Christian parents in Königsberg where he lived for his entire life. His interests were initially in the field of physical science, and it was not until quite late in life that he became interested in philosophy. In 1781, at the age of 57, he presented *The Critique of Pure Reason*. Other works followed such as *Groundwork of the Metaphysics of Morals* (1785) and *Critique of Practical Reason* (1788). At the heart of his thinking was the freedom of the individual. It is, he argued, man's inner reasoning that dictates his moral

actions. These actions, motivated by the mind's reasoning, are free actions, and it is this freedom that he must accord his fellow man regardless of status, colour or creed. Kant called this universal rule of action a 'categorical imperative'. 'Act only on that maxim that you will to be a universal law!' Kant stated the categorical imperative another way: 'So act as to treat humanity, whether in thine own person or in that of any other, in every case as an end withal, never as means only.' Kant died after a long illness in 1804, but his writings were to influence philosophers throughout the 19th century. Hegel and Marx drew on some of Kant's ideas in developing their systems of philosophy, and the existential ethics of Sartre and de Beauvoir in this century rely heavily on Kant's philosophy.

References

Firth, R. (1952), Ethical Absolutism and the Ideal Observer Theory, *Philosophy and Phenomenological Research*, Vol. 12, pp. 318–319.

Henderson, V. (1977), *Basic Principles of Nursing Care*, Geneva: ICN.

Meltzer, M. (1975), *Never to Forget: The Jews of the Holocaust*, New York: Harper & Row.

United Nations, *Declaration of Human Rights*.

Further reading

Benjamin, M. and Curtis, J. (1981), *Ethics in Nursing*, New York: Oxford University Press. See in particular Chapters 1 and 2 on 'Moral Dilemmas and Ethical Enquiry' and 'Unavoidable Topics in Ethical Enquiry'. This book adopts a case study approach to ethical issues, applying various theories to the questions under discussion.

Fromer, M.J. (1981), *Ethical Issues in Health Care*, St. Louis: C.V. Mosby. See in particular references to 'utilitarianism' (p. 27) and 'natural law' (pp. 170–171).

Hursthouse, R. (1978), *Introduction to Philosophy*, Open University Arts Foundation Course, A101, Units 13, 14 and 15. Milton Keynes: Open University Press. See in particular Unit 14, Part 2, on utilitarianism.

Warnock, G.J. (1967) (reprinted 1982), *Contemporary Moral Philosophy*, London: Macmillan. See Chapter 2 for a useful introduction to the arguments surrounding 'intuitionism'.

2

CULTURAL INFLUENCES ON ETHICAL DECISION MAKING

As we saw in the previous chapter, no two peopi will necessarily agree about the rights and wrongs of any particular action. There are several reasons for such differences of opinion. Our judgements are influenced by many different factors, not least the cultural background in which we live and have grown up. In this chapter I intend to examine some of the major ideological influences, namely, the Judaeo-Christian tradition, Islam, Hinduism and Marxism. In just one chapter of a book it is obviously impossible to give a full account of any of these; each in itself would provide sufficient material for a whole book. I will therefore concentrate on those aspects of each tradition which have a bearing upon ethical issues in health care.

The Judaeo-Christian tradition

Judaism and Christianity have much in common, much of Christian ethical teaching having its roots in Judaism. There are however some differences, and within Christianity some quite distinct differences between the two main traditions of Catholicism and Protestantism. Thus it is possible, and quite common, for Christians to disagree with one another about many ethical issues. I shall therefore attempt firstly to outline some of the key elements which are common to Judaism and Christianity and then those which are peculiar to each tradition.

The common core

The common core of Judaic and Christian ethical teaching is to be found in that section of the Bible known by Christians as the Old Testament. Perhaps the most well-known biblical ethical code is the ten commandments, though it is important to remember that the ten commandments form only a small part of the total picture. While the ten commandments are common to both Judaism and Christianity, the way in which they are interpreted varies. We already saw in Chapter 1 that the commandment 'not to kill' has been differently interpreted throughout the centuries. Furthermore, for the Jew, the ten commandments and other early ethical writings have to be viewed in the light of the Talmud,[1] and for the Christian in the light of the New Testament and subsequent Christian documents.

One thing that Judaism and Christianity have in common is a belief in the sanctity of life. Life is seen as a gift from God and therefore something which man should respect. Similarly, there is a belief in the authority of God, that there are God-given laws which should be adhered to. The debate is about how those laws should be interpreted and, particularly within the Christian Church, how God's law can be discerned. Nevertheless, there is for the Jew and the Christian a framework on which to base moral decision making in life in general and in the specific area of medical ethics. Both traditions are frequently at variance with the Hippocratic tradition which is of course neither Christian nor Judaic in its origins.

Judaism

The Jewish medical ethic is firmly interwoven into the religious tradition. It is not a professional code in the sense of a code drawn up by and for members of the medical profession. It is frequently given explanation and definition by the rabbis, who, while being extremely knowledgeable about Jewish theology and general moral teaching, may have little specific knowledge of medicine.

The essential elements of the medical ethic have been summed up by Jacobovits (1978) as follows: the sanctity and dignity of human life; the duty to preserve health; uncompromising opposition to superstition and irrational cures (including faith healing); a rigid code of dietary restraints and sexual morality; and strict instructions on the rights of the dead.

The emphasis placed on the value and sanctity of life cannot be overstated. Judaism totally rejects any compromise, including those of the Hippocratic and Christian traditions. No distinction is made between natural and artificial, ordinary and extraordinary, and heroic and non-heroic measures to preserve life (Rosner, 1979). So imperative is the injunction to preserve life that it takes precedence over almost all ritual commandments. Indeed, it is a moral duty to disregard ritual laws when they conflict with immediate claims of life or health. 'It is religious precept to desecrate the Sabbath for any person afflicted with an illness' (Orah Hayim, 2, 3338). The only laws which remain inviolate are those prohibiting idolatry, incest, adultery, and murder.

To take life is wrong, as too is any act which might hasten death. The Jewish physician is bound to always strive to preserve life. To withdraw treatment from a patient who is dying is generally held to be wrong, although there is some debate about this. The Jewish rabbinic tradition recognizes a state called *gesisah*. This is defined as a stage in which the patient has become moribund and death is imminent. At this stage it is permitted to withdraw an impediment to dying. There is argument as to whether medical therapies which prolong dying can be considered as hindrances to dying.

Not only is it the duty of the physician to preserve life. The obligation extends to the patient. The patient has a duty to preserve his own life and does not therefore have the right to refuse life-preserving treatment, from which it follows that an individual would be acting wrongly if he or she failed to seek medical treatment if there was good reason for suspecting the existence of a life-threatening disease.

A Jewess would, for example, be under a moral obligation to seek medical attention if she discovered a lump in her breast, and having done so would be morally bound to undergo whatever treatment the physician prescribed, provided such treatment was aimed at preserving life. Some Jewish authorities would go so far as to say that if a patient refused life-saving treatment then this should be forced upon him. The Jewish position is thus in dramatic contrast to that of the patients' rights movement, the latter becoming quite widely accepted in modern Western thinking.

Equally strong in Judaism is the duty to heal. This extends responsibility of the physician to include not only situations which threaten life, loss of limbs or serious impairment of health, but also much less grave situations requiring medical intervention to relieve symptoms or promote well-being. This latter point is remarkable when, for the most part, the medical and nursing professions have only this century begun to lay emphasis on health promotion and prevention of ill health. For the Jew it has been a long-held moral duty.

The Judaic laws governing diet and sexual morality are well known. While to 20th century liberal thinkers these rules may appear rigid, reactionary and even nonsensical, many of them are based on sound practical reason. The rules governing the slaughtering of animals and preparation of animal flesh for human consumption, for example, make sound sense when one remembers they were made by a people living in a very warm climate before the coming of refrigeration techniques. Meat prepared in this way would not turn bad so quickly. The strict code governing sexual morality would prevent unwanted pregnancies and the spread of sexually transmitted diseases. Such laws are too a natural progression from the main underlying belief in the sanctity of life and the duty to preserve life and promote well-being.

Since 1953 when the Israeli Government passed the Anatomy and Pathology Law there has been, in Israel, a heated medical ethics debate, not over subjects which have caused controversy in other parts of the world (e.g. such issues as euthanasia, abortion, contraception) but over postmortems. The argument is between Israeli physicians who seek to advance their knowledge from postmortem examinations and the Orthodox Rabbinate which is concerned to maintain the traditional Jewish respect for the corpse.

Traditional Jewish moral teaching places strong emphasis on care of the newly dead. This involves far more than rituals to be observed when laying out the body. In *Orthodox* Judaism the body is held to be divine property and not merely the physical remains from which the soul has departed. No one, neither the State, the medical profession nor any other human agent, has the right to use the body for any purpose. Thus, not only are postmortems prohibited but so too are organ transplants. This respect for the dead body seems now to be unique to Judaism, but for many centuries it influenced Christian moral thinking. The battle over postmortem examinations, which followed the 1953 Act in Israel, was fought in the Christian world in the 16th century. Still today some Christians might find it difficult, even impossible, to accept the idea of organ transplants.

Jewish moral law does allow this rule to be overridden in certain circumstances. The requirement to save life can overrule the rules governing the dead just as it can most other moral rules. Thus an organ may be removed from a dead body to save the life of an identifiable sick person. There would be no question of allowing organs to be removed and kept on ice for use when needed. To the non-Jew this would seem to be a ridiculous contradiction. Rabbis will allow heart transplants to be performed, because the heart is going to a known sick person and the action is life-saving, but not allow corneal transplants for these are seldom life-saving.

Catholicism

Catholic medical ethics are extremely complicated. Most people are probably aware of some general moral rules that exist within Catholic moral theology. The proscription of, for example, contraception, abortion and euthanasia is well known. However, the teaching is not that simple. Abortion in the course of certain life-saving treatments is permitted as an incidental effect, i.e. when abortion of the fetus is not the goal. Acts which some would call euthanasia are also allowed. Catholic medical ethics are based on two main components: 'a set of principles derived from the more general theory of Catholic theology and a more problem-oriented set of rules and insights to help people make decisions about ethical problems. This second component is often called casuistry' (Veatch 1981).

The central core of Catholic moral teaching is natural law, but it is a particular understanding of natural law. The natural law is God-given and can be discovered by man through the use of reason. This creates a problem in that since human reason is imperfect then our knowledge can never be perfect. Natural law can, it is held, be reasoned from understanding inclinations. For example, man is inclined to procreate so it must be natural law that he should. It is also held that natural law is confirmed by divine revelation. Thomas Aquinas summed up natural law as 'good is to be done and promoted, and evil avoided'. From this generalized law are derived principles which help to provide answers to specific moral questions. There are five main principles.

Stewardship. Life is given by God and therefore belongs to God. No one is owner or master of his own body. Humans are stewards of their bodies; that is to say they have a duty to care for their bodies and protect both body and soul, from which it follows that one has an obligation to seek medical aid when something goes wrong with that body. It also logically follows, though is frequently overlooked, that each has a responsibility not to behave in a way which will damage the body, and take appropriate action to prevent ill-health. It could be argued from this principle that it is immoral to smoke. Certainly the Roman Catholic Church has always argued that excessive consumption of alcohol is wrong, and of course gluttony is one of the seven deadly sins.

Inviolability of human life. This second principle derives from the assumption on which the first is based. Since life belongs to God, it is sacred and inviolable. It has given rise to the idea of a right to life, but it does not indicate a right to surrender life. What it in fact means is that no one has the right to take my life and nor do I. Rights in Catholic thought are inalienable; they can neither be confiscated nor surrendered. From this principle are derived the specific rules about such acts as abortion, euthanasia and suicide. However, they are not all absolute rules – there are some limits. For example, Catholic moral theologians have argued that there is such a thing as a just war, or that to kill in self-defence is justified, and some that even capital punishment is justified. The reasoning behind this latter point is that the life being taken is not an innocent life and therefore can be said not to be murder, which is by definition the killing of the innocent.

It should be noted here that the basis of these first two principles is totally at odds with modern Western secular ethics and the argument that 'it's my body anyway'.

Totality. Given that the body belongs to God, and is in effect only on loan to the individual, how can surgery be justified? Surely the logical deduction from the first two principles would be that any interference involving the removal, mutilation or destruction of part of the body must be wrong. The problem is overcome by the principle of *totality*, according to which each part only exists for the good of the whole. Thus if an organ is diseased and thereby endangering the whole it may be removed.

The principle applies only to the individual body. It cannot be extended to sacrificing an individual for the sake of society. It does not therefore justify experimentation on humans for the good of society, nor the removal of an organ from one person to another. Nor does it justify the removal of a live fetus from a mother in order to save the mother's life. Such an act would be the destruction of one human life for the sake of another.

Sexuality and procreation. Throughout its history, Christianity has had problems in coming to terms with sexuality and defining the function of marriage. Saint Paul was generally opposed to the idea of marriage and the nearest he ever came to endorsing it was to say, 'It is better to marry than to burn' (1 Corinthians 7, 9).

In Catholic moral theology, marriage has two prime functions. The first is the procreation and nurturing of children, and the second, the expression of love between a man and a woman. Until recent years more emphasis has been placed on the first function rather than the second, the second being for the good of the individual while the first is 'primarily for the good of the species'

(Kelly 1958). Thus follows quite naturally the prohibition on sterilization and contraception.

What then if a woman has cancer of the uterus and the only way to save her life is by removing it? To do so would accord with the principle of totality but contravene the principle of sexuality and procreation. Strangely enough, Catholic moral theologians would justify removal of the uterus and do so even if the woman was pregnant. They would do so on the grounds of the fifth principle.

The principle of double effect. This principle, which has been discussed in Chapter 1, is one which many ordinary people have come to by intuition. Catholic moral theologians have 'taken this intuition to a point of scholarly precision and elegance' (Veatch 1981). The circumstances that have to exist to justify what would normally be considered an immoral act have been discussed in the previous chapter. Here it is sufficient to point out that this principle allows Catholic thinkers to justify acts which would normally be proscribed by one or more of the other four principles.

In cases where there is debate or uncertainty recourse is to the authority of the Church.

Protestantism

While Catholic ethics are complex, Protestant ethics, at least Protestant medical ethics, are vague. While Catholic ethics are based on clearly defined principles, Protestant ethics tend to rely on broad theological themes on which to base individual decisions. In the more general field of morals Protestantism does provide well-defined rules. These rules, such as those relating to sexual behaviour, murder, and property, are based upon biblical teaching. When it comes to the more specific area of medical ethics there are no such rules, largely because the answers to the problems posed are not to be found in the Bible. To answer such questions Protestant ethicists refer to two theological themes which emerge from scripture – covenant and agape or love.

Covenant is based on an ethic of keeping promises. The idea of a covenant relationship can be traced back to the Old Testament. One of the main themes in Old Testament theology is that of the covenant relationship between God and his chosen people. Protestant theologians have extended this to encompass relationships between people, in particular between one member of the Body of Christ (the Church) and others, both individually and collectively. In becoming a member of the Church a person enters into a covenant relationship with God and with his fellow Christians. This imposes on him certain duties and obligations, in particular to be faithful and loyal. Some Protestant theologians have argued that this idea of a covenant relationship can be applied in all human relationships, including that of a professional with a lay person. There is debate as to whether the covenant relationship between doctor and patient is reciprocal or unilateral. Some would argue that while the doctor or other professional, having agreed to accept the patient or client, enters into a covenant or contract to benefit the patient or client, there is no reciprocal obligation on the part of the patient or client to do anything. Others have argued that the relationship, once entered into, binds both professional and client and imposes upon both certain duties and obligations. The professional is bound to benefit the client, the client is bound to accept the advice and instructions of the professional.

Agape or *love* is a central theme of all Christian theology. Ramsey (1970) refers to it as 'a moral quality of attitude and of action owed to all men by any man who steps into a covenant with another man'. The problem is in deciding what is the loving action in any given situation. Some, such as Fletcher, have argued that the loving act is the one which will produce the best consequences, an idea which closely resembles that of Aquinas, of doing good and avoiding evil.

How can one decide what is the loving thing to do in any given situation? Take, for example, the case of a new-born child who is severely physically and mentally handicapped. It could be argued that the loving thing to do would be to actively assist in the child's death, thus sparing the parents much anguish and hardship in the long-term and, although it is much more difficult to determine, saving the child from suffering. To do so would of course contravene the commandment not to kill, and may actually cause the parents to suffer anguish as a result of guilt feelings. What is impossible to be certain of is the degree, if any, of suffering that the child might undergo if allowed to live. The answer probably is that in such a situation whatever decision is taken would be judged on its motives and that neither would be condemned.

It should be pointed out, however, that although there is this strong inclination in Protestantism toward judging every case individually, there is no more question of giving authority for deciding medical ethics to the profession than there is in Judaism or Catholicism.

Islam

Islamic ethical teaching has been influenced by a number of other cultures, among them Greek, Jewish, Christian, Indian and Persian. Nevertheless, although strands of these various cultures can be detected there is a distinct Muslim belief system. The summary of the Muslim faith, 'There is no god but Allah, and Muhammed is Allah's apostle', lies at the core of all Islamic ethical teaching. From this basic affirmation naturally stems the notion that in all things *Allah's will be done*. There is a certain fatalism about the Islamic approach to life. Whatever action humans take, including the skilled intervention of doctors and nurses, at the end of the day the outcome will be as preordained by Allah. If it is Allah's will the patient recover then he will, with or without treatment, and if it is Allah's will that he die then he will, however skilled the physician.

This anti-interventionist attitude, which is never taken to the extreme of totally forbidding any kind of human intervention in the natural state of affairs, gives rise to objections to some medical procedures. Muslim ethicists raise strong objections to anatomical dissection and organ transplants, though partly on the grounds that they would have some effect on life after death. Birth control too creates a moral problem, not for the same reasons as in Catholicism but because fertility is generally viewed as being something which is in the hands of Allah.

The following is a translation from the Koran by Pickthall (1953): 'Whoever killeth a human being for other than manslaughter or corruption in the earth, it shall be as if he had killed all mankind, and whoso saveth the life of one, it shall be as if he had saved the life of all mankind.' Thus actively ending the life of a handicapped child, such as that referred to earlier, is strongly forbidden, as is euthanasia and presumably so too would be assisting another by providing them with the necessary knowledge of how to do so.

This attitude of non-interventionalism linked to a fatalistic approach leads not surprisingly to quite contradictory views. Some Muslim authorities have argued, for example, that contraception is allowed, since fertility is in the hands of Allah, and so whether conception will result from coitus is determined by Allah and the use of contraceptive measures is irrelevant. Muhammed himself is reputed to have said of coitus interruptus (the major method of contraception at that time), 'Do as you please, whatever God has willed will happen, and not all semen result in children' (Musallam 1978).

From this, one might be forgiven for deducing that Muslims are left either with permission to do almost anything, because whatever one does cannot effect the outcome, or with innumerable situations in which one cannot know how to act. Neither is in fact the case. Islamic teaching lays down some very firm and definite laws, e.g. the prohibition on alcohol, laws relating to sexual morality and the rights and duties of individuals in relation to their superiors, especially of women to men. In cases where there is doubt or argument as to the morally right action then recourse is to the religious authorities, and, as in Judaism, it is the religious authorities and not the physicians who rule on ethical issues in medicine.

Hinduism

Hindu medical ethics predate Christian and Muslim ethics and can be traced back to the first millennium BC. Obviously the medical ethics of India today have been influenced by Western thought, but traditional themes still predominate.

The first such theme is the *doctrine of reincarnation*. It is held that one's condition in the present incarnation is the result of one's actions in a previous incarnation. This has implications for medical ethics. The *Caraka Samhita*, one of the earliest medical writings, includes a list of people whom the physician should not treat, including those who are extremely abnormal, wicked, and of miserable character and conduct. The extremely abnormal would presumably include those with severe congenital handicap.

The second theme is the *proscription against killing*. While the *Caraka* forbade the treatment of patients on the point of death (cf. the Jewish notion of gesisah), there is in Hinduism a great respect for life. Active euthanasia is most definitely ruled out.

A third, and perhaps most important, theme is the principle of *ahimsa* which incorporates the notion of non-violence and even the concept of non-hatred. The adoption of ahimsa into central Indian thought is partly due to Buddhism, and has also begun to influence Western thinking. It requires the physician to place more importance on preventing harm than doing good. Non-intervention is justified on the grounds of non-violence, even if intervention may lead to benefit. Thus to take the life of a patient in order to relieve even the most extreme suffering would be wrong, because to take part in the violence of killing is wrong whatever the circumstances. Less dramatically, it would justify non-intervention in the case of an 81-year-old diabetic with a gangrenous toe. Amputation would bring the potential benefit of delaying the patient's death, but would in itself be harmful and cause potential suffering. Not to amputate would be in accord with the notion of non-violence and also the maxim that to prevent suffering is more important than doing good. It could of course be argued that not amputating might lead to excruciating pain and therefore that amputation is justified on the grounds of preventing harm.

Marxism

There are two main differences between Marxist or Communist medical ethics and those so far discussed. One is that in Marxist thinking there is no supernatural deity. The supreme authority is the State. The second, and here Marxism differs from Western secularist as well as religious theories, is that emphasis is placed on the physician's responsibility to the State rather than the individual patient. The Soviet doctor pledges 'to keep and develop the beneficial traditions of medicine in my country, to conduct all my actions according to the principles of the Communist morality, and to always keep in mind the high calling of the Soviet physician, and the high responsibility I have to my people and to the Soviet government' (The Oath of Soviet Physicians).

The Soviet psychiatrist is thus justified in treating as mentally ill persons whose 'illness' is *political*, and who in other societies would not be classified as mentally ill. There is however increasing evidence to suggest that Soviet physicians themselves are becoming less happy with this state of affairs.

What justifies actions in Communist thought is the extent to which they serve the end of bringing about a socialist society. Morality is not absolute or constant but changing, depending on the state of society. Thus Communist ethics change depending on whether the country is in a prerevolutionary, revolutionary or post-revolutionary situation. Yet a further code of ethics applies in a developing country.

In most Communist countries today the moral code is almost puritanical, loose morals being associated with capitalist decadence.

But the overriding purpose and direction of the whole ethic is the building of a Communist society, not that acts are right or wrong in themselves but only in as much as they serve that end. If the individual citizen is bound to act always in ways which will benefit society, the State has a duty to protect, care, and provide for its citizens.

With regard to health care, all have a right, legal and moral, to free and comprehensive health care, and the State (and therefore those involved in its provision) a duty to provide that care. It is much more difficult to discern what the Communist judgement would be in relation to specific issues, largely because the rules and the way in which they may be interpreted can change overnight.

Summary

In this chapter I have attempted to outline some of the main ethical themes pertaining to the major world religions and philosophies. What begins to emerge from even so brief an account are some common and some divergent elements. In all the schools of thought discussed in this chapter the authority from which moral guidelines and rules are drawn is outside or distinct from the individuals involved in the situation. For all the religions the authority is God or some spiritual authority which stands outside the world, and for Marxism it is the almost depersonalized State or Party. Whereas for the religions the rules are for the most part constant, though their interpretation may vary, for Marxism the rules themselves are subject to change. Even so, within each of the belief systems, an individual faced with a moral dilemma has recourse to some authority, either religious or party ethicists and philosophers, who can interpret the general rule as it applies to the situation.

The four religions discussed in this chapter have in common a respect for individual human life which, although expressed differently and arrived at by different routes, leads to similarity of teaching in respect of specific issues. Marxism is often at variance with the religions over specific issues. One main reason for this is that while there is respect for human life it is more a respect for human life en masse rather than individually. The well-being of an individual may be secondary to the well-being of society.

Consider again the case of a new-born child with severe mental and physical handicaps. Possible responses to this situation might be as follows. None of the religions would consider the notion of taking deliberate steps to end the child's life. The Judaic ruling, and probably the Catholic ruling, would be that efforts should be made to keep the child alive. Protestant, Muslim and Hindu would probably all favour non-intervention, though for differing reasons – the Protestant on the grounds that to take no action to actively end or preserve the child's life would be the most loving thing to do, but that the child should be given tender loving care; the Muslim on the grounds that it is Allah's will whether the child should live or die; and the Hindu on the basis that the child is as it is because of its conduct in a previous incarnation and so falls within the category of persons whom the physician should not treat. A Marxist could well justify deliberately ending the life of the child on the grounds that its survival would in no way benefit society, indeed would place an unnecessary strain on society's resources.

Any one of us might agree with any or none of these responses, and our response may coincide with that of a different religion or culture to our own. The reason is of course that most people arrive at moral decisions by their own reasoning processes and may be influenced unconsciously by schools of thought of which they have no formal knowledge, so interwoven have the cultures of East and West become.

Notes

1 The *Talmud* is a compilation consisting of the Mishnah, or accepted body of traditional law, together with the subsequent discussions or traditions concerning it which arose in the Jewish 'schools'. There are two Talmuds: the Palestinian and the Babylonian. In common usage reference is usually made to the Babylonian, which is fuller than the Palestinian. It more or less acquired its present shape about AD 500.

References

Aquinas, T. *Summa Theologica*, I–II, Q94, Art.2, translated. In Gilbey, T. (ed), *The Dominican Fathers of the English Province* (1966), Cambridge: Black Friars.

Fletcher, J.F., cited in Veatch, R.M. (1981), *A Theory of Medical Ethics*, New York: Basic Books.

Jacobovits, I. (1978), Judaism, *Encyclopedia of Bioethics*, p. 792. New York: Free Press.

Kelly, G. (1958), *Medico-moral Problems*, St. Louis: The Catholic Hospital Association of the US and Canada.

Musallam, B. (1978), Religious Traditions: Islamic, *Encyclopedia of Bioethics*, Vol. 3, pp. 1264–69. New York: Free Press.

Orah Hayim, 2:338, cited in Jacobovits, I. (1959), *Jewish Medical Ethics*, New York: Bloch Publishing.

Pickthall, M.M. (1953), *The Meaning of the Glorious Koran: An Explanatory Translation*, Ch.5, v32. New York: Mentor Books.

Ramsey, P. (1970), *The Patient as a Person*, New Haven: Yale University Press.

Rosner, F. (1979), The Jewish Attitude towards Euthanasia. In Rosner, F. and Bleich, J.D. (eds), *Jewish Bioethics*, New York: Sanhedrin Press.

Veatch, R.M. (1981), *A Theory of Medical Ethics*, New York: Basic Books.

The Oath of Soviet Physicians, *Journal of the American Medical Association*, 1971, Vol. 217, p. 834.

Further reading

Baelz, P. (1977), *Ethics and Belief*, London: Sheldon Press.

Jacobovits, I. (1959), *Jewish Medical Ethics*, New York: Bloch Publishing.

Kamenka, E. (1979), *Marxism and Ethics*, London: Macmillan.

Manson, T.W. (1960), *Ethics and the Gospel*, London: SCM.

Sampson, A.C.M. (1982), *The Neglected Ethic – Cultural and Religious Factors in the Care of Patients*, Maidenhead: McGraw-Hill.

Smith, W.C. (1962), *The Faith of Other Men*, New York: Mentor Books.

Reich, W.T. (ed) (1978), *Encyclopedia of Bioethics*, New York: Free Press.

3

SANCTITY OF LIFE VERSUS QUALITY OF LIFE

In this chapter two possibly contradictory positions are discussed; *sanctity of life* and *quality of life*. The implications of each for the provision of health care are explored and the question 'Can they be reconciled?' considered.

Sanctity of life

As we began to see in the previous chapter, the notion of the sanctity of life is central to all religious or theological ethical codes. As Fromer (1981) states, 'the sanctity of life is related to the question of a divine presence'. If one believes in the existence of a divinity and that life is something which is given by that divinity, then one accepts the idea that individuals have no right to end life and a duty to preserve life. A rigid application of this notion would mean that in no circumstances should action be taken to end life and that in all situations every effort should be made to preserve it. However, as we have already seen, such a literal interpretation is adopted by a minority. Even within the Catholic tradition there is some room for manoeuvre, and in the other religious traditions there are exceptions made.

Before looking at the questions to which a code of ethics based on the sanctity of life gives rise, it is useful to explore the notion itself in more detail.

The notion of sanctity

The first point to which we need address ourselves is the meaning in this context of *sanctity*. *The Concise Oxford Dictionary* definition of *sanctity* is 'saintliness; sacredness; inviolability'. The two words given that are relevant to this discussion are *sacredness* and *inviolability*. Anything which has sanctity is firstly sacred, that is to say *holy* and of the divine. It is something which therefore demands respect, even adulation. The problem is that all these words – sanctity, sacred, holy – are part of religious language. They have little meaning outside that context, and the concepts which they embody are only meaningful to those with a sense of the religious. They are totally meaningless to the person who has never encountered the religious.

Inviolability causes less problems inasmuch as it is meaningful to the religious and non-religious alike, though the two might disagree about the precise meaning of the word. For the religious, inviolability is closely associated with the notion of sacredness. Something which is inviolable is something which should not be profaned. A more general meaning of inviolable is *unbroken*. The religious might say that the laws of God are inviolable – they cannot or must not be broken. The non-religious might use the word when talking of the laws of the State. Thus to talk of the inviolability of life, i.e. state that life is something which should not be destroyed, is not essentially a religious notion. It is not necessary to believe in a divinity to believe in the inviolability of life, whereas to talk of the *sanctity* of life, with its wider connotations of sacredness and holiness, is essentially a religious notion.

A phrase frequently used by ethicists and philosophers is *respect for persons*. Kant maintained that human beings should be treated as ends in themselves and never merely as means. The word 'respect' is used here in an almost technical sense. It means 'that any person, as such, has intrinsic worth or value irrespective of his achievements, which in the dealings of other persons with him, may be neither ignored or discounted' (Harris 1966). Thus people of varying or no religious beliefs might unite in condemning the sort of experimentation on human beings described in Chapter 1 on the grounds that it was treating men and women as if they were not persons.

What life?

When we talk of the sanctity of life, what life are we talking about? Is it all life or some life? If we are solely concerned with human life then the question is what constitutes human life? Or if we talk about respect for persons, what is a person?

Some would argue that it is life itself, in whatever form, that is sacred. In Hinduism, for example, there is a strong respect for all forms of life and a repugnance about taking the life of any animal, even of the lower orders. There are those, including some who have no religious belief, who will eat no flesh because they feel that it is wrong to destroy life.

Generally speaking, when the phrase 'sanctity of life' is used, as, for example, within the context of health care, it refers to human life. The area of debate which remains is about what constitutes human life. The questions raised cover the whole life range, from the debate as to when the life form *in utero* can be said to be human, through how near *normal* the being should be, to the debate as to when does human life cease. The debate about life *in utero* will be dealt with in Chapter 7. The question which concerns us here is essentially about what distinguishes human life from other life forms. For the religious believer the answer is the soul or spirit. For the non-religious it is the ability to reason. Man is different from the animals, even the most intelligent, because he has a spiritual component, or because he is capable of rational thought, or both of these elements.

Religious and non-religious agree that man's capability for rational thought distinguishes him from other life forms. A non-religious person might well argue that a being which, to all intent and purpose, looks like a human being but has lost or, in the case of congenital handicap, never had the ability to reason is not human. Its life is therefore not inviolable. The religious argument would be that although that particular attribute of humanness was missing, another essential element, i.e. the spiritual, remains and therefore the life is still inviolable. The religious standpoint is quite categorical. A human being consists of three facets, *body*, *mind* and *spirit*, of which the most essential is the spirit. However deformed the body and however disturbed the mind, even if the mind be totally inactive, as long as the spirit remains it is still a human life and is sacred and inviolable. The spirit continues to live on when death occurs. If it were possible for the body to continue to live after the spirit had departed then it would no longer be human and therefore not inviolable. The belief is of course that the spirit or soul becomes disassociated from the body at the moment of death and it is impossible to conceive of a spiritless or soulless being.

The non-religious does not accept the existence of the spirit or soul but sees humanness as consisting of just two facets, *body* and *mind*. It is a mind capable of reasoning which sets man apart from other forms of life. Thus it is argued that once a person has lost that essential component of humanness, i.e. a rational mind, then he ceases to be human. There is no compunction to preserve such a life. The emphasis is placed very much on the rational mind as opposed to the physical body, though some would argue that it is the combination of the two which make a human being and that severe physical deformity, just as much as a deformed mind, is a criterion for judging a life to be less than human.

So we begin to see that even though religious and non-religious might both lay claim to a belief that human life is inviolable they are nevertheless poles apart. For the religious, a life which is the product of human procreation is born with a soul and is by definition human. For the non-religious, even though a child be born to human parents it may be considered less than human if it does not possess the essential elements which constitute humanness. Judgements are being made about the quality of life.

Quality of life

The phrase 'quality of life' is much used in health care these days. Nurses frequently state that their aim in caring for a particular patient is 'to improve his quality of life' or 'to maintain his quality of life'. The problem is how can any of us really know what is another's quality of life? Any judgement we make is inevitably largely subjective. In effect, what we do is ask ourselves how we would feel if we had that particular physical disability. How would it affect our life? How would I feel if I could no longer remember things as well as I do now? How horrible it would be to have the mental ability of a six-year-old.

A person who has all his mental capacity but is severely physically disabled is able to judge his own quality of life. A person whose mind is malfunctioning may not be capable of such a judgement but, because of his condition, he may be totally unaware of his own limitations. The child born with, for example, Down's syndrome might be judged by the onlooker to have a very poor quality of life. The child himself may be quite satisfied and contented. We can of course never really know since we are not able to get inside someone else and experience life as he does. The elderly person who is suffering from senile dementia has a quality of life which to the onlooker is very poor and by comparison with his previous state is greatly diminished. But again we cannot know what it is like to be that person and of course he cannot tell us. We do not always know if such people are aware of their condition or if they remember what their life was like in the past.

I don't feel my age – so my old age is not something that in itself can
teach me anything. What does teach me something is the attitude of
others towards me. Old age is an aspect of me that others feel. They
look at me and say 'that old codger' and they make themselves
pleasant because I will die soon and they are respectful. My old age is
in other people.
Jean Paul Sartre at the age of 80

Within a nursing context we need to find some criteria with which
to measure a patient's quality of life. Several models are available to
us: Virginia Henderson's 14 basic needs and Nancy Roper's 12
activities of daily living are two such models. These provide a basis
for assessment of the patient's ability to cope with living and provide
guidelines for deciding the intervention necessary to improve the
quality of life. Thus when a nurse writes that the aim of nursing care
is 'to improve the patient's quality of life', she can define this more
specifically in terms of objectives based on such criteria. There is no
suggestion in all this of moral decision making. The nurse so far is
attempting to make an objective measurement of a patient's quality
of life in order to identify the most appropriate nursing intervention
to improve or maintain that quality. If on the basis of the assessment
the nurse was to make a decision about the *value* of intervening then
a moral element is introduced into the process.

Models such as the two to which reference has been made could be
used to determine which lives are capable of being enhanced and
which are not, and hence which lives warrant intervention and
which do not. One could, for example, say that persons unable to
meet less than a specified number of needs had a quality of life which
was so poor as to render that person's life of little value. It should of
course be pointed out that the originators of any of the models used
in assessing nursing needs have never suggested that their models
could or should be used in this way. I merely introduce them here to
illustrate the difficulties involved in first assessing a person's quality
of life and, secondly, making a judgement about the value of a life on
such a basis.

In the practice of health care delivery there are occasions when
decisions have to be made where some criteria for measuring the
quality of life are used. Consider the following examples.

Example 1. If there are two patients, each suffering from the same
disease and requiring the same treatment, but there is only sufficient

equipment or sufficient dosage of a drug for one, then a decision has to be made as to which patient should receive it and which go untreated.

Example 2. Suppose you are a nurse in a small casualty department and you are the only nurse on duty when two casualties are brought in. Both need immediate life-saving treatment. You can only treat one at a time and whichever you treat first the other will quite likely die or at least suffer some permanent disability.

The first situation is one which doctors frequently face particularly in countries where resources are limited but also in more affluent countries with regard to highly specialized and technological treatments, such as transplant surgery or renal dialysis. Usually in such situations there is time to think, time to weigh up various arguments. In the second situation the nurse does not have time; the decision has to be made quickly or both patients may die.

In trying to find solutions to these problems we begin by wanting to know more about the patients involved; their ages, marital status, do they have children, what are their occupations, their levels of intelligence and so on. In other words we want information which will enable us to make a comparison either between the quality of life each might have if treated or the contribution they might make to society. We are trying to place a value on them as individuals – the one with the higher score wins!

On a wider scale, similar decisions have to be made about groups within society. Given that resources are limited, those involved in health care planning are faced with deciding which services for which groups should have priority. Do they spend x pounds on a heart transplant unit which will save a dozen or so lives a year, or spend that same sum on providing more general surgical units and so enable several hundred people to have hernias repaired? Do they spend more money on acute services at the expense of the elderly or mentally handicapped? These are all moral questions. However much we try to rationalize our answers, at the end of the day we are making judgements based on a set of values. In the choice between heart transplants and hernia repairs one could argue that treatments which are life-saving have a higher value than those which are aimed at improving the quality of life. In deciding between acute services and geriatric or mentally handicapped services the case is less clear-cut. It comes down to making a generalized comparison of the relative quality of life of two or more groups of people. The resultant quality of life of the younger group following surgery is likely to be better than that of those in the other two groups, however much services are improved. It is of course not a fair comparison to make. It is based largely on assumption rather than scientific measurement.

The problem is that (as suggested at the beginning of this section) one cannot know for certain what the quality of life of another is. Those who have the responsibility of making such decisions would fall mainly into the first category, i.e. those likely to place demand on the acute services; some might fall into the second group (the elderly), but none into the third group (the mentally handicapped). Thus their judgement about what constitutes a good quality of life is clouded by their own expectations and experiences. As a young middle-aged and reasonably healthy man with full use of all my senses and faculties I consider my quality of life to be most satisfactory. If I were no longer able to read, enjoy music, communicate with others, move about or care for myself, then I suspect my quality of life would be much poorer. I *suspect* that such would be the case; I cannot *know* until, or if, I have the experience. Therefore, I can easily fall into the trap of suggesting that someone who cannot do or enjoy things I do and enjoy cannot have such a good quality of life. In fact that other person might consider his quality of life to be more than satisfactory. Those things which are important to me may be of little or no importance to another.

To have some means of measuring quality of life can be of great value in determining health care but it can also be very dangerous. It is one thing to use it as a basis for deciding the most appropriate intervention, it is another to use it as a basis for deciding the comparative worth of individual lives. It becomes even more dangerous if used to determine whether the life is human or sub-human. The justification of the black slave trade, and it was justified by generations of Churchmen and others, was that the African native was *sub-human*. It was even believed by some that he had no soul. Hitler and the Nazis justified their experimentation on, and extermination of, the mentally handicapped and Jews on just the same grounds. Because so much emphasis is placed on man's ability to rationalize, then it follows that reduction or loss of that ability renders the life of less worth; it may be not even human. As we shall see in Chapter 6, this line of argument is one of those used in defence of euthanasia.

Contradictory or reconcilable?

We now have to consider the question, 'Can these two standpoints be reconciled?' At face value it would appear not. In the practice of health care to some extent they have to be. Occasions arise, albeit infrequently, when a decision has to be made between saving one life and another. The response of a person of the sanctity-of-life school would say that our nurse in the casualty department should make every effort to save both lives. Some would argue that if as a result both died no blame could be ascribed, because the intention was right and all possible effort was made to effect that intention. Others would say that it was better to save one life than none.

Let us assume that in reality the nurse has two choices; to do nothing, in which case both will die, or to attend to one patient. It is obviously difficult, if not impossible, to justify not treating either. She is therefore left with the decision of which patient to treat first, bearing in mind that meanwhile the other may well die. She can make that decision on the basis of two ideas: either which has the higher possibility of survival or which is likely to have the higher quality of life. If the former option is unclear then she must resort to the second. She may hold a very strong belief in the sanctity of life but is here making a decision based on quality of life. The example is of course a dramatic one; nevertheless it does serve to illustrate the point that the two notions can be reconciled.

The sanctity-of-life approach does not, as proponents of the quality-of-life ethic would suggest, deny the importance of the quality of life. The sanctity-of-life approach argues that the quality of all lives suffers if life itself becomes violable. Unless every human life is considered valuable because of its very existence then the quality of life itself is devalued. It is when questions arise as to whether or not to preserve a life that the two schools of thought may be at odds with one another.

Summary

We have in this chapter explored two apparently contradictory standpoints. Both are valid and useful positions on which to base ethical decisions in health care although both do have their limitations. Neither can provide all the answers and, as I have tried to show, they are not necessarily mutually exclusive.

One of the problems encountered if one tries to base all decisions solely on the notion of the sanctity of life has already been discussed, i.e. how to make decisions between two or more lives. It has also been argued that if one pursues the idea rigidly then one may well be guilty of inhumanity. Hence the Catholic teaching on *extraordinary means* of treatment. The traditional stand has been that while there is a moral duty to employ all ordinary means one is quite justified in not employing extraordinary means. The problem today, with rapid advances in medical knowledge and treatment, is deciding what constitutes extraordinary means. Varga (1980) suggests the terms *useless* and *useful means* as being better for moral decision making in health care. It would be quite in accordance with a belief in the sanctity of life to not employ useless means of treatment. I am not totally convinced that the terms 'useless' and 'useful' are appropriate in ethical decision making. They are themselves value judgements and give rise to further questions.

If the notion of sanctity of life does not provide us with a basis for all decision making then nor does the quality of life. The major problem, as we have seen, is in determining what the quality of life of another is. If all the decision making in health care were to be based on the notion of the quality of life it is questionable whether many of the major advances of this century would ever have been made. 'Belief in the sanctity of life is the reason why health care exists and the reason why we are all concerned with the improvement of that care and its provision to all who want it' (Fromer 1981).

It is probably reasonable to assume that most of the health care systems which 20th century man has inherited came into being at a time when there was a fairly generally held belief in the sanctity of life. The implication of Fromer's statement, which I would question, is that we owe health care solely to a belief in the sanctity of life, and that had the only belief been in the quality of life then there would be no health care. My own view is that a belief in the quality of life would have led to the inception of a health care system, but that its scope and development would probably have been very different.

References

Fromer, M.J. (1981), *Ethical Issues in Health Care*, St. Louis: C.V. Mosby.
Harris, E.E. (1966), Respect for Persons. In De George, R.T. (ed), *Ethics and Society*, London: Macmillan.

Henderson, V. (1977), *Basic Principles of Nursing Care*, Geneva: ICN.
Roper, N. (1976), cited in Roper, N., Logan, W.W. and Tierney, A.J. (1981), *Learning to Use the Process of Nursing*, London: Churchill Livingstone.
Varga, A.C. (1980), *The Main Issues in Bioethics*, New York: Paulist Press.

Further reading

Campbell, A.V. (1975), *Moral Dilemmas in Medicine*, Edinburgh: Churchill Livingstone. See Chapter 5 on 'Respect for Persons'.
Fletcher, J.F. (1974), Four Indicators of Humanhood – The Enquiry Matures, Hastings Centre Reports, Vol. 4, No. 6, pp. 4–7.
Schweitzer, A. (1970), *Reverence for Life*, translated by Fuller, R.H, London: SPCK.
Waddams, H. (1972), *A New Introduction to Moral Theology*, London: SCM. See Chapter 9 on 'The Sanctity of Life'.

4

FOR THE GOOD OF WHOM?

In the earlier chapters the questions with which we were chiefly concerned were 'What is right?' and 'How do we know what is right?' The question which underlies the discussion in this chapter is 'Why should we do what is right?', or, put another way, 'Why be moral?' For some people the answer appears obvious – 'because God says so'. Alternatively, as was discussed in the latter part of Chapter 2, 'because the law, the State or some other authority says so'. These sorts or responses to the question 'Why be moral?' come generally within the school of thought known as *authoritarianism*.

The child who asks why he should behave in a certain way may be told by his parent, teacher or some other authority figure 'because I say so'. Such a response does not really answer the question, it merely begs further questions. Why do you – God, parent, teacher, government – say so? What is the purpose of behaving in this rather than that way?

At the risk of over-simplifying the various philosophical responses to these questions I have divided them into two groupings: those whose basis is individualistic, i.e. where the purpose is to benefit an individual, either self or others, and those whose basis is societal, i.e. where the purpose is to benefit all or a large proportion of mankind. Actions might be good because they serve self-interest, or the interests of others (*altruism*). The theories discussed in this chapter are all essentially *teleological* (from the Greek *telos*, meaning purpose) or goal-based theories.

Self-interest

One response to the question 'Why be moral?' might be to say 'because to behave in accordance with what I consider to be right or moral will benefit me'. The benefit may be immediate – I will feel good, it gives me pleasure – or long-term, e.g. in the next life.

One theory which judges the rightness or wrongness of acts in terms of an immediate or short-term reward is *hedonism*. Hedonism, as an ethical system, dates back to ancient Greece. Arristupus (circa

435–circa 356 BC) is thought to have held that an act is good when it is capable of producing sense pleasure. Arristupus and his followers equated sense pleasure with happiness. According to the hedonists, happiness is the goal of man and any act which brings one closer to that goal is good. Conversely, any act which causes pain or reduces happiness is morally bad. The early hedonists realized that a surfeit of sense pleasure is not necessarily a good thing; it may in fact cause pain and boredom. They were in no way condoning the excesses of pleasure seeking, of drunkenness and debauchery which heralded the decline of the Greek and Roman Empires. They recognized that moderation is the rule in all things and that it is a wise man who knows how to exercise sufficient control and avoid becoming a slave to pleasure.

Later Greek philosophers developed this theory further. Epicurus (341–270 BC), for example, also identified the goal of man with pleasure but emphasized rational rather than sense pleasures. Rational pleasures are those such as peace of mind, friendship and intellectual pleasures. Thus acts which increase these pleasures are morally good while those which do not, or prevent them, are morally bad. Aristotle (384–322 BC) advanced a similar view and claimed that it pays to be courageous, generous or temperate because these types of behaviour alone give one a sense of happiness in one's relationships with others. A virtuous man is a happy man.

Consider for a moment how many times you have heard, perhaps used, such phrases as 'honesty pays', 'do as you would be done by' and other similar clichés. Why does honesty pay? Presumably because in the long run you will benefit by it, you will earn trust and respect and avoid getting into trouble – 'be sure your sins will find you out'. If you are kind and helpful to others then they in return are more likely to be kind and helpful to you.

The dishonest man may argue differently. He might say 'Look where your honesty has got you; you are poor and taken advantage of by others, whereas my dishonesty has brought me wealth and power.' He might well conclude 'dishonesty obviously pays'. Provided his dishonesty is not discovered, and also bearing in mind that not all forms of dishonesty are illegal, he might go from birth to death without receiving any form of punishment. He might go on to say that he has no objection to others behaving dishonestly so long as in doing so they do not harm him. Thus 'do as you would be done by' or 'treat others as you would have them treat you' – what is known as the *Golden Rule* – while providing a convenient and practical guide to daily moral decision making is not without criticism. It is based on the supposition that all men have the same nature, the same needs and desires.

Most religious ethical codes are teleological and to a greater or lesser extent appeal to one's self-interest. The reward is not the immediate pleasure of the hedonists but something in the future. The promise for those who obey God's will is eternal life or, for those who believe in reincarnation, a better existence next time. The question asked of Jesus by the young man was 'Master what good must I do to gain eternal life?' (Matthew 19, 16). The answer was 'Keep the commandments'. In the ensuing discussion the nature of the commandments and the moral behaviour that would bring about the reward was spelled out. There was no question that to seek eternal life was a right goal. The notion that the goal of morally good behaviour is eternal life is frequently emphasized in the ethical teaching of Jesus.[1]

There is a tradition of thought which is to be found in many religious and cultural traditions. This tradition holds that man's goal is self-fulfilment or self-realization. Any action which brings one closer to that goal is good while any action which deflects from it is bad. This is as true of the early Christian hermits who sought a closer relationship with God as of the Buddhist monk, or the Hindu who leaves his family to sit at the feet of a guru.

Altruism

Altruism, meaning regard for others as a principle of action, is an integral component of many ethical codes. I am sure that many people reading the preceding paragraphs would say 'That's not true. I am not kind to others in order to obtain some reward, I do it because I want to benefit them.' Or 'I behave in this way because it will benefit mankind as a whole or the society in which I live.'

For the benefit of the individual

The response of many Christians to my earlier contention, that the reason for being kind, generous and caring to others is to inherit eternal life, might be that the reason for so acting is to demonstrate to those others the love of God and so bring them into the Kingdom. Similarly a person with no religious conviction might argue that they behave in this way because they value that person as an individual, as a fellow human being. This leads to the maxim that in our relationships with others we should act in their best interests. The question then is who decides what is in another's best interest.

For the person with a strong religious or ideological conviction the answer might be that they *know* what is another's best interest or that the answer is to be found in the doctrine of their belief. The danger here is one of self-contradiction. For if one holds that each person is an individual, that he has an intrinsic value as an individual, and that he has the same ability as oneself to reason and choose, then by deciding for him what is in his best interest is to deny him his individuality and value as a person. This was certainly the error committed by, for example, many Churchmen and Churchwomen in Victorian England. It gives rise to a *paternalistic* approach which, until recent years, typified doctor-patient, doctor-nurse and nurse-patient relationships – the doctor/nurse knows best!

I used in describing this particular stance the word 'error', which is to make a value judgement. Not all would concur with my view that paternalism is a bad thing. 'I do not want to go along with a volunteer basis. I think a fellow should be compelled to become better and not let him use his discretion whether he wants to get smarter, more healthy or more honest' (General Hersley).

In recent years the trend in nursing has been away from *telling* the patient what is best for him and what he should do toward *involving* him in the decision making process. It is inherent in the approach to nursing known as the *Nursing Process* that the patient, and his family, have a right to and should be encouraged to be involved in identifying his needs and planning the programme of care, and a right to make moral decisions. The philosophy which underlies the Nursing Process is:

● that people are individuals;
● that, while recognizing certain basic human needs which are common to all, each individual has needs and problems which are peculiar to him;
● that patients have rights over their own bodies and to have a say in what is done to and for them.

This naturally gives rise to what is sometimes described as individualized nursing care. From the patient's viewpoint this is doubtless a good thing, for no longer is he *a patient* who has had an appendicectomy and therefore has known problems common to all patients following that operation and for which there are laid down nursing procedures, he is now *Mr Albert Brown*, aged 46 years, married with two children and employed as a bricklayer. He has a range of needs and problems some of which he shares in common with others following an appendicectomy but also some of which are peculiar to him because he is who he is. The nursing care can no longer be standard or routine but has to be planned for and with him.

Once we begin to consider patients as individual human beings then we have to accord them all the rights we accord to any human being and perhaps additional rights because they are patients. In recent years, the patients' rights movement has gathered momentum and this has greatly affected not only nursing attitudes but also those of the other health professions. Rights-based theories and how rights are determined will be discussed in the next chapter. At this point what concerns us are the implications of the notion that patients have rights as patients.

One obvious implication is that the professionals are more likely to have their decisions questioned by patients. If this, as in many instances it has, leads to the profession re-examining its own standards of practice, the body of knowledge on which its members have based their decisions and its values, then the effect must be for the better.

Another implication, perhaps less desirable, is that placing emphasis on the rights of the individual may lead to conflict. If there is one nurse to one patient or one doctor to one patient then such statements as 'the patient has the right to considerate and respectful care' (American Hospital Association 1972) present little difficulty. Indeed there would probably be general agreement among nurses that all patients do have such a right. But what if the patient is one of 40 elderly men, many of whom are confused, noisy, demanding or incontinent and there are just two nurses on duty for the night? Considerate and respectful care implies considering the patient's particular needs, taking into consideration that he is slow to understand or slow to move, respecting him as a fellow human being and paying him the common courtesy of stopping to listen to him. To afford all this to the patient in the first bed might be to deny it to the other 39. Therefore, the nurses have to make decisions about priorities. They have to decide which patients have priority and which needs of individual patients are more or less immediate.

There comes a point in all aspects of life when the needs and rights of the individual have to be considered in the light of the whole. Consider again the ward with 40 elderly patients and two nurses. Three patients have very definite and urgent needs of which the two nurses are aware: Mr Jones has been incontinent of urine and needs a change of bedclothes; Mr Brown is in pain and has asked for his injection which is due – he also desperately needs to talk about his fears for the future (the two nurses being unaware of the latter need); Mr Smith is confused and noisy. There are obviously more ways than one of dealing with this situation.

It could be argued that the priority is to relieve Mr Brown of his pain, pain being a more acute and distressing problem than incontinence or restlessness. Giving an analgesic requires both nurses to be involved, one to administer it and the other to check it. It is not therefore possible for one nurse to deal with Mr Brown's problem while the other attends to Mr Jones or Mr Smith. In any case both nurses will have to attend to the other two patients. Meanwhile Mr Smith is becoming noisier and other patients are beginning to complain. If, when the nurse gives Mr Brown his injection, he pleads with her to stop and talk with him the problem is compounded.

Another possible answer might be to say that Mr Smith should be attended to first, calmed down and given a sedative; otherwise he is going to disturb all the other patients.

For the good of the majority

Thus we begin to see that the needs of one person cannot in every situation be dealt with in isolation. Mr Brown was one of 40 patients, all with their own needs and all equally entitled to 'considerate and respectful care'. The nurses must apportion their time among all the patients. In such a situation it would seem more appropriate to attempt to meet some of the needs of all, rather than all the needs of some.

As we saw in Chapter 1 some utilitarians would argue that the main principle to be obeyed is to act in such a way as to give the greatest happiness to the greatest number. To some extent utilitarianism is a development and modification of hedonism, for utilitarianism accepts the notion that all men act to gain pleasure or to avoid pain. Jeremy Bentham (1748–1832) and his immediate followers equated pleasure with happiness, and said that the goal of human acts is to achieve the greatest possible happiness. The next step is to decide which acts increase happiness. These are then defined as good acts and those which produce pain are bad acts. Bentham called the property of the act that produces happiness *utility* and hence *utilitarianism* is the name given to this particular ethical theory.

Bentham held that all pleasures can be *quantified* and that therefore it is possible to calculate the greatness of happiness. He argued that men are basically selfish but have necessarily to consider the happiness of others because they need the help of their fellow beings for their own happiness. Thus he deduced that the morally good act is that which produces the greatest happiness for the greatest number of people.

John Stuart Mill (1806–1873), while accepting the basic principles of Bentham's theory, rejected the idea that all pleasures can be measured *quantitatively* and argued that pleasures differ *qualitatively*. Pleasures that befit rational human beings rather than those held in common with lesser animals have greater value. He also placed more emphasis on the social character of happiness than did Bentham. The goal of moral actions is the greatest happiness of all members of society.

Two further refinements of the utilitarian theory are *act utilitarianism* and *rule utilitarianism*. *Act utilitarianism* is so called because it is the act itself that is judged to be good or bad according to whether it serves the principle of greatest happiness. *Rule utilitarianism* tries to establish rules that are capable of producing the greatest happiness for the greatest number. The rules are arrived at by assessing the hypothetical consequences of everyone following a rule that a particular act is to be done or not done. For example, suppose I am a rule utilitarian and I want to decide whether it would be right or wrong to drop my empty drink carton in the street. What I do is ask myself what the consequences would be if everyone followed the rule 'throw your litter in the street if you want to'. Or, more simply 'What if everyone did it?' The consequences would most certainly not promote happiness because the streets would soon become very untidy and hazardous. So the rule is not a right rule and therefore the act is not right. Rule utilitarians insist that rules are universally binding. Thus if the rule is 'to throw litter in the street is wrong' then no one is exempt from that rule. One person dropping one piece of litter in the street detracts from the cleanliness of the street and therefore from the greatest happiness.

There is therefore a fundamental difference between act and rule utilitarians, although both agree that the goal is the greatest happiness. Act utilitarians, because they judge each act by its consequences, may well judge an act to be right on one occasion but wrong on another. One would expect rule utilitarians to say that if the rule is that the act should not be done then it is never justified whatever the circumstances. In practice though, rule utilitarians are not so rigid – they do not hold all rules to be sacrosanct.

Consider, for example, the question of keeping promises. The rule is 'keep promises'. Breaking promises is wrong because if everyone did so it would cause the whole institution of keeping promises to break down and that would certainly not promote the greatest happiness. Therefore one might think that rule utilitarians might claim that this rule is sacrosanct. Of course to do so would be to afford to promise keeping more importance than it deserves.

Suppose Jane has promised to meet her boyfriend outside the cinema at seven o'clock and further promised that for once she will not be late. On her way to the cinema Jane sees an accident – a small boy is knocked from his bicycle by a speeding car. The driver does not stop and the boy is lying in the road. He is crying and Jane can see blood on his face and hands. There is no one else around. What is the right thing for her to do?

An act utilitarian would have no hesitation in saying Jane should stop and attend to the boy even though this means she will be late for her meeting and will therefore have broken her promise. If the rule 'keep promises' were sacrosanct then the rule utilitarian would have no option but to say 'no, she should keep going and keep her promise'. That is obviously nonsense. Keeping a promise about meeting a friend is not as important as saving someone's life. The rule utilitarian's response would be to point out that 'preserve life' is a good moral rule. Obviously if everyone obeyed the rule it would increase human happiness. What he has to do in this case is to appeal directly to the greatest happiness principle, and clearly life saving will lead to greater happiness than promise keeping. In this particular case the act and rule utilitarians would be in agreement.

In providing a framework for moral decision making, utilitarianism and rule utilitarianism in particular, can be very useful. However, there is a flaw in the argument. Utilitarians base their argument on several suppositions. Firstly, they presuppose that everyone knows what the happiness or well-being of man is and that everyone understands it in the same way. If, as the utilitarians claim, everyone can estimate what actions promote happiness then each individual could set his own criterion of morality. The result would be chaos, which of course rule utilitarianism attempts to overcome. Another supposition is that everyone becomes happy in the same way, in other words that acts which are anticipated to produce the greatest happiness will be pleasurable to individuals. Yet man's experience has shown that the best interests of the majority of people are not always served by such acts, nor do individuals always find their consequences pleasant.

The questions which, it can be argued, utilitarians have failed to answer satisfactorily are 'How can we know what happiness is?' and 'How can we determine the best way of achieving it?' Nevertheless in some situations the notion of the greatest good or happiness for the greatest number can be a useful guide to decision making.

In the example discussed earlier of the ward with 40 elderly patients this idea would enable the nurses to come quickly to a decision. The decision to deal first with Mr Smith would be a *right* one. In doing so, Mr Smith and 37 other patients in the ward would benefit. Quiet would ensue and they would be able to get to sleep. It would of course not meet the primary needs of Mr Brown and Mr Jones. So we come to another flaw in the utilitarian's argument; for in striving to attain the greatest good for the greatest number one might totally ignore or violate the interests of the minority and, in some cases, the minority might be quite a sizeable portion of the whole. The utilitarian's answer to this objection is that if the application of a rule had this effect then the rule would not be morally good because it would violate the fair and equal distribution of goods. In so doing utilitarians are contradicting the moral criterion of utilitarianism by appealing to a more fundamental standard, that of justice.

For the good of all

In Chapter 2 we saw that in Marxist ethics the criterion by which acts are judged as right or wrong is the extent to which they serve the interests of the State. It could be argued therefore that the concern was not for the good of the majority but for the good of all, or at least the whole population of the State. So on the face of it Marxist ethics are aimed at achieving greater benefit than are utilitarian ethics. In practice of course 'for the good of the State' is not the same as 'for the good of all citizens', because what the Marxist is more concerned about is preserving the structure of the State rather than its contents. It may, for example, serve the best interests of the State to dispose of a section of the population. Certainly it means that there is no responsibility to act for the good of those outside the State.

The effect of applying Marxist ethics is to totally ignore individual needs and differences. It may lead, as does utilitarianism, to violating the interests of the minority, even those of the majority. Of course Marxist theorists would argue that in the long term anything which benefits the State will benefit the whole population, but the population it will benefit is in the future and not the present.

Is it possible then to talk of a code of ethics which seems at all times to benefit all? Some religious theorists would answer in the affirmative. Christians, for example, would argue that the ultimate goal is to bring all mankind into fellowship with God. What justifies any act is the extent to which it promotes that goal.

Summary

In this chapter we have been concerned with teleological or consequential theories of ethics, where the criterion for moral decision making is the effects or consequences arising from an act. Essentially the various theories discussed can be divided, as I have done, into two categories: those whose consequence is individual good and those whose consequence is the good of the majority. They could as well be divided into selfish and altruistic theories.

If one tries to base decisions in nursing or health care generally on the extent to which acts will benefit the individual then this can lead to better patient care. It may however mean better care for one patient to the detriment of others. So while the growth of individualized patient care might be welcomed because it treats the patient as a person rather than as one of a number of cases, it may lead to conflict within the minds of the providers of care. If resources are limitless then there may be no problem. In practice, resources, including those of the individual carer as well as those of society, are limited. Care then has to be apportioned and priorities identified.

To base decisions on the criterion of the greatest good for the greatest number becomes a very attractive idea. It provides both the individual carer and policy makers with a yardstick. However, as we have seen it does have its flaws primarily because it involves a large element of subjectivity.

The underlying question which has concerned us in this chapter is 'Why be moral?' The theories discussed have all attempted to provide an answer, be it for benefit of self, of other individuals, or of the greatest number. In the next chapter we will still be concerned with the same question but will look at theories which attempt to answer it from a different starting point.

Notes

1 See for example: Matthew, Ch. 19, v27–29; Matthew, Ch. 5, v1–10; Matthew, Ch. 5, v17–19; Mark, Ch. 12, v28–34; Luke, Ch. 6, v20–23.

References

American Hospital Association (1972), *Patients' Bill of Rights*.

Gospel According to Matthew, Ch. 19, v16 ff. New English Bible. Oxford: Oxford University Press and Cambridge University Press.

General Hersley, quoted in Dworkin, G. (1976), Paternalism. In Gorrovitz, S. et al (eds), *Moral Problems in Medicine*, Englewood Cliffs, N.J.: Prentice-Hall.

Further reading

Baelz, P. (1977), *Ethics and Belief*, London: Sheldon Press. See in particular Chapter 5 on 'Why be Moral?'

Bayles, M.D. (ed) (1968), *Contemporary Utilitarianism*, New York: Doubleday.

Gorrovitz, S. et al (eds) (1976), *Moral Problems in Medicine*, Englewood Cliffs, N.J.: Prentice-Hall. See in particular Chapter 1, extract from 'Utilitarianism' by John Stuart Mill and Chapter 2, essays on 'Paternalism'.

Smart, J.J.C. and Williams, B. (1973), *Utilitarianism – For and Against*, Cambridge: Cambridge University Press.

Reich, W.T. (1978), *Encyclopedia of Bioethics*, New York: Macmillan and Free Press. See especially the following articles: 'Ethics: Teleological Theories', Kurt Baier; 'Ethics: Utilitarianism', R.M. Hare; and 'Paternalism', Tom L. Beauchamp.

Thompson, I.E., Melia, K.M. and Boyd, K.M. (1983), *Nursing Ethics*, Edinburgh: Churchill Livingstone. See in particular Chapter 5 on 'Moral Dilemmas in Nursing Groups of Patients.'

5

DUTIES, RIGHTS, RESPONSIBILITIES

In the preceding chapter the theories discussed judged the rightness or wrongness of an action by its goal. The answer to the question 'Why be moral?' was 'In order to achieve the goal'. The theories discussed in this chapter are not concerned with the goal but more with the act itself. The answers to the question are 'because we have a *duty* to be moral' or 'a *right* to expect morally good behaviour from others' or 'we have a *responsibility* toward others'. The act is good in so far as it is in accord with the duty, right or responsibility.

In Chapter 2 we saw that in Judaic law, for example, the physician has a *duty* to treat, and the patient a *duty* to accept treatment; while in Marxist thought there exists the notion that all have a *right* to health care. Professional codes of ethics frequently contain statements which begin 'The *professional* has a responsibility to . . .' The RCN Code of Professional Conduct discusses the *responsibility* of the nurse 'to patients or clients', 'for professional standards' and 'to colleagues'.

These ideas of duties, rights and responsibilities are frequently applied in all aspects of living. People talk of the duties of parents toward their children, the duties of citizens to report crime, the rights of individuals to education and free speech, and the responsibilities of families for their own members, or of governments toward the citizens of the country.

Before examining theories based on these concepts in more detail it is helpful to try and clarify more fully how they differ from those discussed in Chapter 4. *Teleological*, or goal-based, theories are concerned with the consequences of the act. It is the goal which determines whether the act or rule is morally good or bad. The theories discussed in this chapter can for the most part be grouped under the heading *deontological* (Greek, *deon* = duty). The consequences of the act become almost immaterial. What determines if an act is good or bad is whether or not it conforms to our duty or obligation. Thus in judging rightness or wrongness of actions we are examining the opposite ends of the sequence of events. Figure 1

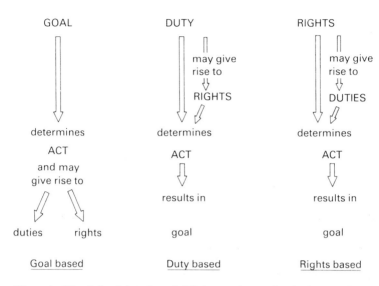

Figure 1 The chain of thought and differing emphases of goal-, duty-, and rights- based theories.

illustrates the different emphases between goal-, duty-, and rights-based theories.

The goal might be the same in all three situations but that which determines the right act varies. If one begins by defining the goal one might arrive at a set of duties and rights which are in accord with those of duty- and rights-based theories. It may not necessarily be so, for as we saw in Chapter 4, if the goal is the greatest happiness this does not always lead to a duty to be unselfish. Conversely, if one starts from the point that one has a duty to be unselfish it will almost certainly maximize happiness, at least if happiness is equated with rational pleasure.

From Figure 1 it can be seen that in goal-based theories the goal is the primary factor while any duties or rights derived are secondary. In duty-based theories, where the duty becomes the primary factor, the goal is of secondary importance. Duties may give rise to rights and vice versa. For example, if I have a *duty* to tell the truth then this gives rise to the idea that you have a *right* to be told the truth. Similarly, if you have a *right* to free speech then I have a *duty* to allow you that.

Duty-based theories

In utilitarian ethics, the end justifies the means. What duty-based ethics do is place a limit on the means while not necessarily disagreeing with the goodness of the end. For example, if the duty is to preserve life, then that is binding. One cannot turn round and say 'but in this particular circumstance the goal (greatest happiness) will be best served by not preserving life'. The duty remains a binding duty even if in acting in accordance with it will do nothing to achieve the goal, or even detract from its achievement.

What can exempt one from acting in accordance with a duty is the obligation to act in accordance with another. It is fairly generally agreed by all duty theorists that to tell the truth is a basic duty. However, one would be justified in not telling the truth in order to comply with the more important duty to preserve life. One would be quite justified in telling a lie in order to prevent the death of another. This is somewhat of a simplification of the position. There might be situations in which truth telling would take precedence over life preservation. Consider the following situation. Suppose you witness a murder and the only penalty for murder in your country is execution. Would you be justified in telling a lie or at least failing to tell the truth in order to save the life of the murderer?

Kant's view of duty was that of the categorical imperative – 'Act only on that maxim that you will to be a universal law'. Kant held that consequences are relatively unimportant but that one has an obligation to act in a particular way because one has a moral duty to do so. Any act performed from a sense of moral duty is morally worthy and, he concluded, can cause no harm. This is fair enough if duties are clearly defined and agreed by all, for then there can be no dispute. The Kantian view is far less definite. It requires a person to exercise his reason and arrive at a logically sound maxim, as tested by the categorical imperative. However, the categorical imperative is insufficiently informative and the individual is left to some extent to decide what his duty is. The duty once defined becomes binding. This could be dangerous if universally applied in health care.

The problem is that this type of duty-based theory totally disregards the desirability of either the means or the consequences. Any action is justified solely on the basis of conformity or non-conformity to the duty. For example, suppose someone considers he has a duty to eliminate a particular disease, say sleeping sickness. This is obviously a quite admirable idea. One way, probably the only way, to eliminate this disease is to eradicate the cause – the tsetse fly. Again, on the face of it an admirable thought. Suppose the only known way of effectively eradicating the tsetse fly is to spray the marshy area in which it thrives with a poison which, in addition to killing the tsetse fly, will be absorbed by fish and kill other animals and birds who eat the fish. Suppose this act sets up a chain of events. The eradication of the tsetse fly renders the area safe for cattle. The cattle move in and consume the lush vegetation, eventually laying the area bare and causing the creation of a barren dust bowl.

A strict interpretation of Kant's theory would be to ignore these and any other consequences, and justify spraying with this particular insecticide because it is in accord with one's duty. Of course, what one has to do is to consider the action in the light of other duties. Does the duty to eliminate sleeping sickness take precedence over the duty to preserve the life of other species, or to maintain the balance of nature?

It is a fairly commonly held view that a nurse's duty to her patients is paramount: that she should place the needs of her patients above all else including her own needs. It is held that it is in order for a banker to go home at five o'clock even if he has unfinished paper work but the nurse cannot go 'off duty' if to do so means patients' needs will go unmet. This altruistic attitude is a very noble one but it does lead to much conflict and may well be misguided. How much should nurses give of themselves; how selfless should they be and how long should they keep going? In other words, do nurses have a duty, i.e. to their patients, which is greater than their duty to meet the terms of their contract of employment? If they continually neglect their own needs will they in the end benefit their patients?

Rights-based theories

'The question of whether health is a right or a privilege is so old and so often asked that it runs the risk of being a cliché' (Fromer 1981). Before we can begin to discuss rights in health care we need to decide what exactly we mean by a *right*. Generally when we talk of *human rights*, as in the United Nations Declaration, we are talking about natural rights, rights which it is believed exist irrespective of time or place.

Consider these two statements: (a) 'My child has a right to

education' and (b) 'I have a right to send my child to the school of my choice.' Statement (a) is talking about a right which many have come to accept as a basic human right, a natural right. Statement (b) is obviously talking about a different type of right. The speaker may have that right if the government has decreed that its citizens should do so but they do not have this right by virtue of being human. Some would argue otherwise. They would say that the right to choose one's child's school is not so much related to the right education as to another natural right, i.e. the right of free choice.

The right of freedom to choose is a particularly thorny one. There must inevitably be some limits placed upon it, if only because one person's right to choose may impinge upon that of someone else. Consider a somewhat simple example. I might claim that I have a right to do whatever I like in my own home. What then if I choose to regularly invite some musician friends home to play jazz together into the early hours of the morning? My neighbours would doubtless complain that I and my friends were disturbing their peace and preventing them from sleeping. They might claim that they have a right to a peaceful environment, especially if they had chosen to live in the neighbourhood because it had a reputation for being quiet. They could also claim that they have the right to be able to sleep at nights.

So we begin to see that there are different types of rights. Fromer (1981) distinguishes between two distinct categories of rights – *option* rights and *welfare* rights.

Option rights. The right to choose what I do in my own home is an option right. While in theory one has the right to behave as one pleases, there are limits or boundaries placed upon the extent to which one can exercise such a right. Sometimes the boundaries are clearly defined as, for example, in defining acceptable modes of dress or undress in certain circumstances. One is free to wear as much or as little as one likes in one's own home but there are clearly defined boundaries as far as how little one can wear in public. Sometimes the boundaries are less clear-cut, as in the case of my claiming a right to play music whenever and however I like in my own home. Sometimes the rights of one individual overlap with those of another and we have to decide which takes priority.

According to Golding (1978), option rights 'should not be taken as implying a general principle to the effect that one has the right to do as one pleases as long as no-one else is harmed'. Golding goes on to point out that there may be some things to which one has no rights even though they do no harm to others, and equally there may be some things one has a right to do even if they do harm others.

Option rights are essentially concerned with personal freedom but they are not about total freedom; they do themselves involve an element of control. If I have a right to do as I please within the boundary of allowed behaviour, what Fromer describes as my 'sphere of sovereignty', then you have no right to prevent me exercising mine. If my actions go beyond the defined boundary or sphere then you have a right to stop me. Indeed it is option rights which are the basis of most, if not all, suits in civil courts. A sues B because B has either prevented A from exerting his rights, or because A has been unable to stop B when B has gone outside his sphere.

Welfare rights. Welfare rights are rights granted by law. Thus in the United Kingdom, for example, one can claim a right to expect a certain standard of safety in building construction, a right to clean air, a right to a secret vote in parliamentary elections and so on. Conflict arises when individuals lay claim to rights not granted in law but which are an integral part of their own moral code. If sufficient numbers lay claim to a right that does not exist then it might be that they can bring pressure to bear to bring about a change in the law and the creation of a new welfare right. Welfare rights are about benefits or legal entitlement. I have the right to expect something or to receive something whereas, as we have seen, option rights are concerned with personal freedom.

Implications of rights-based theories

The notions of freedom and possession of rights are clearly inter-twined. You cannot have freedom without having rights. Although the reverse is not necessarily true it is possible to accept the idea that people have certain rights without allowing them total freedom. A society might concur with the idea that citizens have a right to education without allowing them the freedom of choosing whether to exercise that right. It might also be held that they have a duty to be educated. Even in a totalitarian state the citizens may have some welfare rights but have little personal freedom. Nevertheless there is a positive relationship between freedom and rights, as Figure 2 illustrates.

Now then, if possession of rights implies freedom it follows that

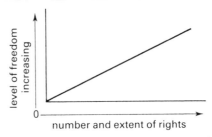

Figure 2   Relationship between level of freedom and the number and extent of rights.

one has the freedom to choose whether or not to exert one's rights. For example, I may have a right, a welfare right, to health care but choose not to request care when I am ill. I have the right not to exercise my right. On the face of it that may appear to pose little difficulty. If I choose not to have my illness treated that is my affair; I might be accused of behaving foolishly but not immorally – not that is unless my not exercising my right prevents others from exercising theirs. It could be argued that if my illness were infectious, in choosing to not have it treated I would be denying those around me the right to live in a healthy environment.

On the other hand if another of my rights, an option right, is freedom of control over my own body, then I have every right to decide what I will allow others to do to it. I have the right to decide whether I want it washed, prodded and examined, massaged, X-rayed, perforated by needles and any of the other things that health workers might want to do to it. It follows that if my decision is to be based on reason rather than emotion I also have the right to be given sufficient information on which to base my decision. And just as I have the right not to exercise my rights I also have the right to do so.

We begin to see that rights, whatever their source or nature, cannot exist in isolation. If everyone based all their actions on their rights and their freedom to choose whether or not to exercise their rights with no concern for others, then chaos would ensue. There is a need for some kind of control. The control may be self-regulating, as is the case quite often with option rights, or it may be a legal one or a moral one.

Let us assume that a government accepts that every child has a right to a free education. The government automatically imposes upon itself the duty to provide the opportunity for every child to receive a free education. There is nothing to stop a child's parents from paying for an education and not exercising the right to a free education. Nor is there anything to stop them from not exerting their right in another way, by opting out altogether. Obviously if everyone chose the latter course the result would be disastrous and, even if a few chose it, it would be less than desirable. The government can of course manipulate the situation by legislating that parents must ensure their children receive an education and can insist that the free State education will be the only provision.

In this situation the government has defined (a) a right and (b) a duty. The right is a welfare right and the control is a legal duty. However, not all duties are defined by law. The government in recognizing the right of its citizens to a free education automatically becomes duty-bound to provide the means. This is frequently the consequence of accepting rights. Some would argue that it was always the consequence.

Let us return to the question of rights in health care. Earlier I referred to my right as a patient to choose not to seek health care. The extent to which I can exert that right is, I suggested, controlled by the rights of others. It could also be argued that it is controlled by my duty toward others. That is, a moral duty to not act deliberately in any way which will harm others. Obviously if I choose to exert my right to health care it has implications in that someone has a duty to provide it. The implications of my exerting my rights *in* rather than *to* health care are more far-reaching.

'The granting of rights automatically implies corresponding duties and responsibilities; one cannot exist without the other' (Fromer 1981). If a patient chooses to exercise his right to have his treatment explained to him then someone has an obligation to give him the information. The question of information-giving will be explored more fully in Chapter 10. Here we merely establish the consequences of rights-based theories in health care. So let us turn our attention to some other rights. 'I have the right to be free from pain' (*The Dying Person's Bill of Rights*). If a patient has the right to be free from pain then health carers have a duty to keep the patient free from pain. The question which immediately arises is whether it is always possible to keep the patient free from pain. What if no known analgesics are effective or if the only effective ones are unavailable? What if the only way to relieve the pain is to give a lethal dose of a drug?

If a patient has the right to choose whether or not to undergo a particular treatment and he chooses not to do so, then the carer has a duty to allow him that choice. If that choice in no way endangers his life or if it will have little or no effect on the course of his illness or recovery then there is no real problem. For example, if a patient refuses a bed-bath then the nurse would have little difficulty in complying with that decision. What if the patient refuses to undergo life-saving surgery or to have a life-sustaining drug such as insulin?

The answers to questions such as those posed at the ends of the last two paragraphs are two-fold. Firstly, it might be argued that the patient has a duty to promote his own health and therefore to undergo appropriate treatment to that end. Secondly, the health professionals might argue that they have a duty which supersedes all others and that is the duty to preserve life. They therefore have no right to refuse to carry out treatment or to refuse to not carry out treatment which will contradict that duty. They could argue that the patient cannot refuse the treatment or that if he does then their duty is to override the patient's wishes.

The duty to promote one's own health could be said to be derived from a right to health if such a right exists. A right to health is not the same as a right to health care. The latter is becoming a generally accepted right, while the former has not been established and is to some extent an unrealistic expectation. It is not as yet possible for man to prevent or cure all illness. Therefore, the duty to promote one's own health is not derived from a right and is a basic duty.

To rely solely on rights-based theories in making ethical decisions would result in frequent conflict and almost certain chaos. Certainly in the practice of health care it frequently becomes necessary to appeal to some other basis for making decisions. Rights-based theories do not provide a sufficiently structured framework to encompass the whole gamut of moral decisions. Nevertheless, the notion of rights and of natural rights in particular, has brought a vital dimension to the ethics of health care which traditionally have relied heavily on the notion of duties. It is the increasing acceptance of the concept of a right to health care that has brought increased motivation to remove inequalities in health care both within and between nations.

Responsibilities

'The fundamental responsibility of the nurse is four-fold: to promote health, to prevent illness, to restore health and to alleviate suffering' (International Council of Nurses 1973). As already noted, codes of professional ethics frequently contain statements about the responsibilities of the members of the profession. Benjamin and Curtis (1981) describe such statements as that quoted from the ICN Code as *statements of creed*, as opposed to *commandments*, for such statements are not so much directives to behave in a particular way as statements of belief; they are saying something about what the profession believes to be the nature of, in this case, nursing.

'As creeds, codes of nursing ethics provide a valuable reminder of the special responsibilities incumbent upon those who tend the sick' (Benjamin and Curtis 1981). Patients or clients are vulnerable, particularly if they are sick or handicapped. They may be very dependent upon the nurse, not just to provide them with their physical needs but to protect them from abuse or deceit. If as a result of illness the patient suffers a loss of hearing, sight or reasoning power, then he may be frightened and very vulnerable. He may have difficulty in understanding the explanation of his treatment. He may, albeit temporarily, be unable to make a rational and objective choice between alternatives even if he is offered one. The nurse has a responsibility to help the patient understand more fully the information presented to him. However, she should not use her advantaged position afforded her by her knowledge and skills to persuade the patient to make one choice rather than another. As Francis Bacon said 'knowledge is power'. It is a criticism frequently levied at professions that they keep their body of knowledge to themselves in order to maintain, even increase, their power in society.

'The primary responsibility of nurses is to protect and enhance the well-being and dignity of each individual in their care' (RCN Code). Patients are vulnerable not only because of physical or mental impairment. Sadly, nurses and other health professionals frequently increase the patient's vulnerability by reducing, rather than enhancing, his dignity. He is placed in unfamiliar surroundings, i.e. a hospital or clinic. He is required to dress in night-clothes even though it is daytime and even if he is able to be up and about. Most of the conversations between professional and patient take place while the patient is lying on a bed or couch. The professional wears at best normal daytime clothes or at worst a uniform. All these factors only serve to increase the patient's vulnerability. It is almost impossible to converse on equal terms with someone else when you are wearing night-clothes and they are wearing a uniform. It makes it difficult for the patient to ask for explanations of his illness and its treatment. It makes it easy for the professional to tell the patient what is 'best' for him, to take control of him.

Nurses have responsibilities not only to their patients but to the profession and to society as a whole. 'The nurse, midwife or health visitor shall: accept a responsibility relevant to her professional experience for assisting her peers and subordinates to develop professional competence' (UKCC 1984). The nurse has a responsibility not just to ensure that her own knowledge and skills are constantly being improved but also to contribute to the development of knowledge and skills within the profession as a whole. This means that a nurse cannot view her job solely in terms of her direct interactions with patients but has to have regard for the needs of her colleagues. The statement quoted above from the UKCC *Code of Professional Conduct* limits the nurse's responsibility to the profession to teaching her peers and subordinates, i.e. other nurses with whom she is in contact.

Her responsibility to the profession is wider than that. Item 8 of the American Nurses' Association (ANA) Code for Nurses states that: 'The nurse participates in the profession's efforts to implement and improve standards of nursing'. This suggests that each individual nurse has a responsibility not just for local standards of care but for contributing to the enhancement of the standards of the profession as a whole. It seems to me implicit in this statement that nurses have a responsibility to be actively involved in whatever machinery exists for promoting standards of care. This would include active membership of professional associations, full involvement in the organizational structure in which she works, and being engaged in research. It also would seem to imply that her responsibility does not cease with the end of the working day.

The pursuit of enhancing standards of care may well bring an individual nurse into conflict with her colleagues. It has frequently been said that a nurse's responsibility to her profession, or that of any professional to his or her profession, means protecting the profession from criticism. 'Always support your colleagues in public.' Professions, and nursing is no exception, have a tradition of *closing ranks* when faced with criticism from outside. Professions should welcome such criticism, even invite it, and members of the profession should, if they feel the criticism to be justified, add their support to it. If nurses are prepared to question their practices and to explore alternatives then one of the main aims of the profession, i.e. to improve standards of care, will be better served.

It is not only its own actions and decisions which a profession should question but also those of others in as much as they affect its sphere of concern. Thus nurses have a responsibility to society to concern themselves with the decisions and actions of other health care professions, and also those of politicians when they affect the health status and care of the community. If a government cuts the amount it spends on health care or refuses to initiate legislation to decrease environmental pollution then nurses, singly and collectively, ought to have something to say. Indeed, they have a responsibility to society to say it.

Summary

In this chapter we have considered alternative answers to the question 'Why be moral?' The three answers examined have been (a) because I have a duty . . . , (b) because he has a right to . . . and (c) because I have a responsibility. Duties and rights may be natural or basic, i.e. existing as part of the natural order of things. Alternatively they may be contrived, i.e. defined by man or by a particular society. Such duties and rights can of course be as easily abolished as they are created. Both duty- and rights-based theories have made major impacts on the ethics of health care but, as we have seen, neither on their own provides sufficient framework for all decision making.

Whereas duties and rights are an integral part of societal or cultural ethics, responsibilities, as discussed here, are part of professional ethics. Because they are nurses, nurses have certain moral responsibilities that are not shared by other members of society.

References

American Nurses' Association (1976), *Code For Nurses*.

Benjamin, M. and Curtis, J. (1981), *Ethics in Nursing*, New York: Oxford University Press.

Fromer, M.J. (1981), *Ethical Issues in Health Care*, St. Louis: C.V. Mosby.

Golding, M.P., cited in Fromer, M.J. (1981), *Ethical Issues in Health Care*, St. Louis: C.V. Mosby.

International Council of Nurses (1973), *Code for Nurses: Ethical Concepts Applied to Nursing*, Geneva: ICN.

Royal College of Nursing (1976), *RCN Code of Professional Conduct – A Discussion Document*, London: RCN.

UKCC (United Kingdom Central Council for Nursing, Midwifery and Health Visiting) (1984), *Code of Professional Conduct for the Nurse, Midwife and Health Visitor*, 2nd Edition. London: UKCC.

The Dying Person's Bill of Rights, created at a workshop on 'The Terminally Ill Patient and the Helping Person', in Lansing, Michigan, USA.

Further reading

Bandman, B. and Bandman, E.L. (1978), *Bioethics and Human Rights*, Boston: Little, Brown.

Fromer, M.J. (1981), *Ethical Issues in Health Care*, St. Louis: C.V. Mosby. See in particular Chapter 1 on 'Professional Accountability' and Chapter 2 on 'Justice and Allocation in Health Care'.

Reich, W.T. (1978), *Encyclopedia of Bioethics*, New York: Macmillan and Free Press. See especially the following articles: 'Ethics: Deontological Theories', Kurt Baier; 'Health Care: Right to Health Care Services', Albert R. Jonsen; and 'Rights: Rights in Bioethics', Ruth Macklin.

Ross, D. (1969), *Kant's Ethical Theory*, Oxford: Oxford University Press.

Thompson, I.E., Melia, K.M. and Boyd, K.M. (1983), *Nursing Ethics*, Edinburgh: Churchill Livingstone. See in particular Chapter 3 on 'Responsibility and Accountability'.

6

EUTHANASIA

Euthanasia has for many years been a controversial issue both within and outside the health professions, and there exist several misconceptions as to what it actually means. Therefore, before examining the various arguments surrounding the act of euthanasia it is necessary to define what is meant by it.

Definition

The word 'euthanasia' is derived from the Greek words *eu* and *thanatos*, and literally means a gentle or easy death. As such it is probably every person's hope, for while most would not wish for a sudden death nor would they wish for a lingering one. Death which comes peacefully in the night during sleep is what most would hope for themselves, especially if they had been able to prepare themselves for it. A dying man expects his doctor to be able to make death, when it comes, as easy and pain free as possible, and today this is possible in the majority of cases when it is known that death is impending. To this literal meaning of euthanasia there can be no moral objection. However, in modern usage, the word euthanasia has taken on a very different meaning. It has come to mean *the painless killing of men and women to end their sufferings*, and it is often referred to as mercy killing.

It is euthanasia in this latter sense with which we are concerned in this chapter: the deliberate ending of life, either voluntarily or involuntarily, on the grounds of humanity, as distinct from murder which does not generally have the interests of the victim or society at heart. However, this definition requires some further clarification and it is necessary to identify those acts which can or cannot be said to be included within it.

Take for example the case considered in Chapter 1. In that situation the doctor was faced with the decision to give or not to give analgesics, the dosage of which, required to relieve the patient's pain, would inevitably hasten his death. There is was argued that not to give the analgesic would be ethically indefensible, and to do so was justifiable. The question we now ask is 'Can this be called euthanasia?' The answer is *yes* in the literal sense, for what the doctor is doing is relieving the patient of pain and thus making the process of dying easier, but *no* in the sense under discussion here, because the doctor is not deliberately setting out to end the patient's life.

Another act which is often referred to as mercy killing is the decision of a doctor not to resuscitate a patient but allow him to die quickly and naturally. The law, at least in the United Kingdom, does not call this killing, again because the doctor is not deliberately killing the patient. Not to throw a lifebelt to a drowning man would be morally indefensible in the view of the majority of people; whereas not to resuscitate a dying man when to do so would only stave off the moment of death or result in a prolonged and unpleasant death, or a cabbage-like existence, can be morally defended. It can be argued that preserving physical existence when there is no mental or spiritual existence is not preserving human life.

These two types of situations are often referred to as *passive euthanasia*, and it is argued that such acts can be morally justified. My concern in this chapter is less with passive euthanasia and more with active euthanasia. The two ideas can be clearly differentiated. Passive euthanasia can be defined as 'cooperating with the patient's dying' (Nelson 1973), and active euthanasia has been defined as 'those techniques and procedures deliberately intended to interrupt the patient's ability to sustain life, to legalise which an Act of Parliament would be necessary' (Nelson 1973).

The case for euthanasia

In defence of active or positive euthanasia Fletcher (1973) argues that 'It is harder morally to justify letting somebody die a slow and ugly death, dehumanised, than it is to justify helping him to escape from such misery'. Fletcher argues that what we should be concerned with is the preservation of humanness and personal integrity above biological life and function. 'The traditional ethics based on the sanctity of life . . . must give way to a code of ethics of the quality of life.'

Man is more than a biological being; he is a rational being. When the rational element is lost, it is argued, then what is left is less than human. There is therefore no obligation to preserve the life of an individual who has lost cerebral capacity and is no longer able to rationalize or express emotion but is still capable of physiological functioning. Thus, it is argued that it is justifiable to end the life of a person whose ability to reason has been lost, as in the case of a man suffering from severe brain damage as the result of a motor accident, or of a teenager who suffers loss of cerebral function as a result of meningitis, or the child born with severe mental handicap. Such persons are incapable of rationalizing and are therefore not *human*.

Furthermore, since such persons as those described in the preceding paragraph are incapable of rational thought, they would be unable to make a decision for themselves as to whether they should live or die. Someone else would make the decision for them, and would, according to this school of thought, be morally justified in so doing.

Twentieth century man is faced with moral decisions unknown to his predecessors. Advances in medicine and science continually open up new areas of decision making and a greater ability to control the course of nature. Modern medicine has given us considerable control over the birth process, and it has also opened up new possibilities for resuscitation and prolonging life. We are therefore forced into making decisions about death as much as about birth. Those in favour of euthanasia would argue that there must be the same quality control in the terminating of life as in its initiating. 'It is ridiculous to give ethical approval to the positive ending of subhuman life in utero, as we do in therapeutic abortions for reasons of mercy and compassion, but refuse to approve positively ending a subhuman life in extremis' (Fletcher 1973).

Earlier, I argued that there is a very clear distinction between passive and active euthanasia. Many supporters of euthanasia would disagree with such a view. They argue that there is no such moral distinction between the two acts, between letting die and killing. Since the former is accepted in certain circumstances (e.g. a patient on a life support system who stands no chance of recovery) then the latter must also be acceptable. 'There seems in fact to be no general difference between the obligation not to cause harm and the obligation to prevent harm, and no general difference between the obligation to refrain from killing others and the obligation not to let others die. Hence there is little if any basis for thinking that active and passive euthanasia differ in some morally significant way' (Montague, 1978). Therefore it follows that since passive euthanasia is practised and morally defensible, then there is no reason to disallow active euthanasia. The argument of course works both ways; if there is no moral difference between the two then neither should be allowed.

As was discussed in Chapter 1, one way of deciding whether an act is right or wrong is to consider the extent to which the end result serves humane values. Proponents of an end-justifies-the-means ethic would argue that in some circumstances the end (death) does justify the act of deliberately bringing it about. No life, it is argued, is better than dehumanized life. The Hippocratic Oath says nothing about preserving life as such. It says: 'So far as power and discernment shall be mine, I will carry out regimen for the benefit of the sick and will keep them from harm and wrong'. The case for euthanasia depends upon an understanding of *benefit*, *harm* and *wrong*. It can be argued that there are instances in which death may be a *benefit* to the patient, that to maintain life may in fact cause *harm* in so much as the patient is forced to continue a life the quality of which is less than human, and to do so would be *wrong*.

One further argument used by some advocates of euthanasia concerns the rights of the individual. In April 1970 Dr Gray MP asked leave to 'bring in a Bill to make lawful administration of euthanasia at the request of the recipient' (*Hansard*, 1970). Gray's argument rested on the contention that the choice of life or death should always be with the individual concerned. At present, he argued, the decision to prolong life rested with the doctors, and in so doing the doctors were imposing their own value systems on the patient. This, Gray said, offended against the terms of individual liberty. Doctors, he said, fell into three broad categories:

1 those who practised a certain amount of euthanasia already (e.g. by withholding drugs in cases of serious illness);
2 those who did not 'strive officiously to keep alive' the patient according to their own humane values; and
3 those who held that life had an absolute value which in no circumstance must be ended.

Since 1961 it had ceased to be illegal (in the United Kingdom) to take one's own life. Doctors in category 3 might therefore be prohibiting that choice. Similarly a patient who held the absolute values of the third category might be cared for by a doctor in either of the other categories. Legislation allowing voluntary euthanasia, Gray argued, would allow the individual a choice of action which complied with his own set of values. Basically, Gray argued that each individual was entitled to live his life in accordance with his own value system, and that no-one had the right to impose a set of values upon another. This right to live according to one's own values extended to death.

If it is true that every individual has the right to live his or her life according to his or her own value system, then this must also apply to doctors and nurses. One weakness in Dr Gray's line of argument is that had his Bill become law, then society would be requiring doctors and nurses to relinquish the very rights it was seeking to give to patients.

One of the vital differences between man and the animals is that man has the *capacity for death by choice*, and thus the use of this option puts man on an entirely different plane from other animals which we may decide simply to put down when the appropriate time occurs. If a man exercises his *right* of death by choice, he can also donate a vital organ and know that the necessary operation can be arranged in advance and the time of death established without any doubt or difficulty. So to choose the moment of our death when suffering from an incurable disease seems both merciful to the individual and also may be of benefit to others. The *right to die* has become something of a basic principle in the campaign to legalize euthanasia. It is the principle behind, for example, the desire of Karen Quinlan's parents to have the respirator switched off when she had been, for all human purposes, apparently dead for a considerable time, and it is the principle behind the desire to allow sufferers from an incurable disease to say when the time has come to welcome death.

The arguments against euthanasia

Fletcher claims that it is harder to justify letting someone die slowly than it is to give him a lethal injection. His argument is based upon a *personalistic* or *humanistic* code of ethics. He argues that life in itself is not important, that it is rationality and personality that make a person human. While one might agree with him that man is composed of many facets – personal and physical, spiritual and corporeal (or as traditionally described, body and soul) – one might well argue that he overemphasizes the personality and soul to the detriment of the physical. 'To say that existence is not sufficient reason for an individual to be recognized as human is to almost totally exclude the physical dimension of man' (Weber 1973). The body, while it may be a temporary thing, unlike the spirit which may live on after death, is still an essential element of humanness. It is the embodied person with which doctors and nurses are concerned; it is the physical being which is presented to them for their care and treatment. To violate the physical body is to violate the human person as much as violating the personality.

When one thinks of the person as a combination of the spiritual and the physical it is less difficult to differentiate between letting a terminally ill patient die and directly ending the life of a patient. 'The point is, of course, that killing a patient removes his chances of recovery in a way that allowing him to die does not' (Montague 1978). There is a defensible and valid distinction between killing and letting die. Those who would want to prolong life at all costs fall into the trap of placing too much emphasis on the physical, while those who argue in favour of euthanasia frequently place too much emphasis on the personality. It is the needs of the total person we have to consider.

The needs of the terminally ill patient may be best served not by attempting to extend his life, but by concentrating on his needs as a dying person. 'Respect for a dying person may demand that we stop the art of healing so that we can help the patient practise what medieval man called *ars morendi*, the art of dying' (Weber 1973). Active euthanasia is something very different. It is not an attempt to meet the needs of a dying man, but a direct ending of his life, and as such is a violation of the person. Death becomes the result, not of disease, but of the act of a human agent. The difference is a very important one which should not be ignored, for as Weber has it, 'There is an enormous difference between not fighting death and actively putting an end to life. The former is fully compatible with respect for human life. The latter, while done with the best intentions, is logically part of the view that human life itself is not enough to warrant our respect'.

The quality-of-life ethic, when used to support active euthanasia, is in danger of self-contradiction. Those who support such a view are in effect saying that in order to improve the quality of life it may be necessary to destroy it. Furthermore, the case for euthanasia would extend beyond that of the terminally ill patient who has become dehumanized and would, for example, justify the killing of babies born with such disorders as Down's syndrome, whereas the sanctity-of-life approach argues that the quality of all lives suffers if life itself becomes violable. Unless every human life is considered because of its very existence then the quality of life itself is devalued.

In Judaeo-Christian belief, life is sacred and therefore all ethical judgements must be grounded in a reverence for life. Jews and Christians are not, of course, alone in believing in the sanctity of life, but for them there is the added dimension of belief in God as creator. Life is given, and therefore can only be taken, by God. The problem is, as was discussed in Chapter 2, the Bible does not contain mention of specific moral issues such as euthanasia. What it does contain is a set of moral or ethical principles which need to be applied to particular situations. The first basic principle which concerns us here is the commandment 'Thou shalt not kill.' For many, that statement closes the argument. 'Thou shalt not kill', therefore euthanasia is wrong. But, as we have already seen, that commandment has not been taken by all to mean that killing is prohibited in all circumstances. Indeed in some situations it could be argued that the principle not to kill is outweighed by another Christian principle, to show love and compassion. It could be argued that to end the life of a patient was an act of love and compassion, and therefore justified. Proponents of a sanctity-of-life ethic would argue that nothing should or can override that basic principle. Love and compassion for the terminally ill should be directed toward improving their quality of life, and more effort should be given to developing therapeutic techniques.

The second principle on which Christians and others base their argument is the law of nature. 'Some theologians have argued that God's will is reflected in nature and that to act against nature is to act against the will of God. To terminate life, and not let nature take its course, is to act immorally' (Rayner 1976). The obvious flaw in the argument, as Rayner points out, is that it goes too far. Most if not all medical practice is an interference with the course of nature. Were it not for the advances of antenatal care, preventive medicine and antibiotics, many of the now incurably ill would not have survived to contract their present disease. Therefore, since medical interference is partly responsible for the problem it would seem ridiculous not to interfere with nature in order to solve the problem. The argument should not be about whether to interfere with nature, but about the form that interference should take.

With euthanasia, as with many other ethical issues, to argue for it on the basis that the end justifies the means is to place emphasis on the reason for acting rather than on the action itself. 'By concentrating almost exclusively on the proposed end of serving human happiness and well-being, ethicists of the end-justifies-the-means variety seem to forget sometimes that the means chosen can deny the ends desired' (Weber 1973). Fletcher argues that by ending a person's life one can be providing for his well-being. The question is, if he is losing his life, his *being*, can this really be said to serve his *well-being*? It is hard to see how a person's quality of life can be improved by the ending of it.

That those who would support the introduction of legalized active euthanasia are guided by humane and loving motives cannot be denied. Their concern is for the well-being of the individual and the preservation of human dignity. However, while it must be admitted that some patients suffering from incurable diseases do suffer extreme pain, and some do die in agony of body and mind, the question remains whether euthanasia is the best answer to the problem. In recent years, medical science has made great strides not only in heroic life-saving surgery and technological medicine, but also in the less dramatic field of pain control. The work of those involved in the hospice movement has shown that it is possible to control both physical and mental pain even in the terminal stages of malignant disease. While a lot still remains to be done, this surely is the direction in which medicine and nursing should move, for this is working towards a positive solution to the problem, whereas euthanasia is a negative and defeatist solution. It has been shown that death with dignity is possible without resorting to a deliberate hastening of the process.

The *right-to-die* argument is claimed by many to be unfounded, for we have a right to die in as much as it is an inevitable condition of life itself. We do not have a right to choose when or how we will die any more than we can choose when we will be born. True, the former is a technical possibility while the latter is obviously impossible, but ability to do something is not in itself a right to do it. Nor can the right to *die* be compared to the right to *life* of the *Declaration of Human Rights*, for closely bound up in that right to life is that no one has the right to take the life of another. Any form of involuntary euthanasia is thus most definitely not justifiable. Any attempt to choose the moment of our death is really a claim to a right to suicide, and although suicide is not illegal, it is not therefore automatically morally defensible. Nor should a right to die be confused with the genuine, commonsense conclusion frequently reached by doctors that nature take its course and a patient, whose life is being artificially prolonged or who is already dead in effect, should be allowed to die. In fact, in such cases, to prolong life unnecessarily could be said to be interfering with a person's right to die in a more acceptable sense of that phrase – the inevitability of death.

Administering euthanasia – who and how?

So far I have discussed the theoretical moral arguments surrounding euthanasia. There is also the more practical problem of its administration. Who is to carry out any form of euthanasia?

It is often assumed that doctors and/or nurses will do so, but there is a strong body of opinion within both professions against this proposal. The main reason for this is the effect it would have on the doctor-patient and nurse-patient relationship. The relationship between patient and doctor, patient and nurse, is one of trust. The patient entrusts the doctor with his life. He submits to treatment on the recommendation of the doctor in the belief that it will be for his own good. Once euthanasia becomes a legal possibility then the dying patient will become suspicious of any change in treatment, every injection or other form of medication that was prescribed. As Rayner points out: 'Once it [euthanasia] were known to be permitted many patients would fear the most innocent treatment – a pain killing injection perhaps might be an instrument of death; such fear would not only make the patient anxious and hinder recovery, but would introduce a new dimension of suspicion into the doctor-patient relationship' (Rayner 1976).

The other vital question is who should decide whether and when to administer euthanasia. The attempts to legalize voluntary euthanasia in the United Kingdom have left the decision to the patient; the patient deciding well in advance, while still healthy or comparatively so, that should occasion arise when they are dying and in pain or have lost all reason that they should receive a lethal dose of some drug or alternatively the patient being able to request euthanasia when they are suffering from some incurable disease. Those in favour of the former proposition would argue that the decision is made while the individual is still capable of rational decision. The flaw in this argument is that if it is assumed that when in extreme pain the patient is not capable of making a rational decision what happens if, when the moment comes, he changes his mind? Does the doctor ignore this on the grounds that the patient is not capable of rational thought and administer the fatal dose?

The alternative is euthanasia on demand, the patient asking for death when in a state of extreme pain or suffering. Unfortunately, as those who are involved in caring for the terminally ill know, a patient may well ask to die one day but the next day have a strong desire to go on living. Who then would decide whether to act? The plans suggested in the Bills put before the House of Commons in 1963 and 1969 were complicated in the extreme. The complicated legal procedure involved is totally alien to the medical and nursing professions. The whole decision-making process would become so cold and legalistic as to completely detract from the doctor-patient relationship, and there would be little room for compassion in such decisions.

Summary

In this chapter I have attempted to outline some of the main ethical arguments both for and against active euthanasia. I leave it to the reader to decide which is the stronger case. There are, of course, other arguments and viewpoints upon which I have not touched and these would require equally lengthy discussion. Hugh Trowell subtitled his book *The Unfinished Debate on Euthanasia*, and doubtless the debate will continue for many years. While there remain so many doubtful areas and so many unanswerable questions, it would seem wrong to formally allow the practice of active euthanasia.

In order to legalize active euthanasia in the United Kingdom an Act of Parliament would be required. For this to happen it would be necessary to prove that a change in the law would remove greater evils than it would cause. The Working Party of the Church of England's Board for Social Responsibility concluded that such a justification cannot be given.

Case for discussion

Gladys was 58 years old and married to Frank, her second husband. She had two daughters by her first husband, both of whom were married with young children. Gladys was transferred to a Continuing Care Unit from the local general hospital, diagnosed as suffering from an inoperable carcinoma of the colon with a secondary growth in the liver. Initially, she responded well to treatment for pain and symptom control and was discharged home after two weeks.

Two months later she was readmitted in pain. She had lost weight and was jaundiced. Within 48 hours of admission her pain was again under control. She was very much aware of her appearance and this caused her much distress. Gladys frequently asked the doctors and nurses to 'give me something to end it all'. Since she was pain free and reasonably comfortable, oriented and still able to attend to her own personal hygiene, the staff could not understand the reason for her request. Gladys became persistent, and eventually it was discovered that her reason for requesting death was her appearance. She did not want her young grandchildren to watch the gradual, and, as she saw it, horrific deterioration in her appearance.

The staff declined to agree to her request, and she died some two weeks later, quietly and pain free. To the end she continued to make her request that they end it all. Throughout, her husband and daughters had tried to reassure her about her appearance and at no time supported her request to be allowed to die.

References

Fletcher, J. (1973), Ethics and Euthanasia, *American Journal of Nursing*, Vol. 73, No. 4, April.

Hansard, House of Commons, (1970), Vol. 799, Cols. 252–258. (Note: Dr Gray's motion was defeated without a division.)

Montague, P. (1978), The Morality of Active and Passive Euthanasia, *Ethics in Science and Medicine*, Vol. 5, pp. 39–45.

Nelson, J.B. (1973), *Human Medicine*, Minnesota: Augsberg Publishing House.

Rayner, The Most Rev., K. (1976), Euthanasia: A Christian Perspective, *Australian and New Zealand Journal of Surgery*, November, Vol. 46, No. 4.

Trowell, H. (1973), *Euthanasia – The Unfinished Debate on Euthanasia*, London: SCM.

Weber, L.J. (1973), Ethics and Euthanasia – Another View, *American Journal of Nursing*, July, Vol. 73, No. 7.

Further reading

Church Information Office (1975), *On Dying Well*, London: Church Information Office.

Kubler-Ross, E. (1978), *To Live Until We Say Goodbye*, Englewood Cliffs, N.J.: Prentice-Hall.

Saunders, C.M. (1975), chapter on 'Terminal Care'. In Bagshawe, K.D. (ed), *Medical Oncology*, Oxford: Blackwell.

The Linacre Centre, *Linacre Centre Papers*: Prolongation of Life. See Paper 1: The principle of respect for human life (1978); Paper 2: Is there a morally significant difference between killing and letting die? (1978); and Paper 3: Ordinary and extraordinary means of prolonging life (1979).

The Linacre Centre (1982), *Euthanasia and Clinical Practice: Trends, Principles and Alternatives*. The Report of a Working Party, London: The Linacre Centre.

Trowell, H. (1973), *Euthanasia – The Unfinished Debate on Euthanasia*, London: SCM.

7

THE UNBORN CHILD

In this chapter several issues related to the unborn child will be discussed, namely, abortion, *in vitro* fertilization and experiments on embryos. Pertinent to all these issues is the question 'When does human life begin?', and that must be the starting point of our discussions.

The beginning of human life

To some extent the answer to the question will be affected by one's definition of human life and, as we saw in Chapters 3 and 6, there are various definitions. For the moment we can put the question of what constitutes human life to one side and turn to some facts. We know that the development of human life begins with the coming together of sperm and ovum and that it continues through life *in utero* to birth and beyond. 'The continuous and uninterrupted development of the *conceptus* into a newborn child suggest that human life is present from the moment of conception' (Varga 1980). The moment of conception then is one answer to the question of when human life begins.

Others have argued that it begins at different stages of development – the implantation of the fertilized egg in the uterine wall, the commencement of brain activity, the beginning of spontaneous movements of the fetus, viability, even the moment of birth itself. All of these are signs of stages in development. They are all known to occur and can be identified in each individual. None in themselves can really lead one to the assumption that the nature of the fetus has changed, because they are nothing more than signs that the fetus has moved from one stage of biological development to the next. Why should, for example, a non-viable fetus be non-human and a viable one human? Identifying precisely the moment at which the fetus becomes viable is difficult and what is considered viable today was not a hundred years ago.

This capacity to survive independently is contingent upon
technologies and interventions that, at this moment, make the point
of viability somewhere in the area of 20 to 24 weeks in gestation. If,
however, the point of viability were reduced technologically to a much
earlier period, perhaps even to the point of conception, holders of the
viability position would logically have to shift with the state of the art.
Veatch 1981.

Again, why should a viable fetus be non-human but a newborn child
human?

While science provides us with valuable information about the
development of a human being from conception to birth it cannot
pin-point the moment at which human life begins, the reasons being
that, with one possible exception, those attributes which are said to
be essential elements in defining human life are not measurable by
scientific means. If human life equals the capacity to become a
rational, self-determining being, then that the capacity is there in the
unborn child is to some extent supposition. It is only when the being
has developed those attributes that we can say retrospectively that
the potential was there all along.

If what distinguishes human life from non-human life is the
presence of a soul or spirit, then again we cannot know whether or
not the soul is in the unborn child. There is no scientific measurement or test to prove its existence.

Actual possession of the ability to reason can be tested, but only
once the child has developed communication skills to such a level as
to be able to demonstrate that ability. Indeed, some would argue that
the ability to reason occurs at quite a late stage of development and
one is left with the obviously nonsensical idea that human life begins
at some stage after birth. The question 'When does human life
begin?' is not a scientific one but a philosophical one.

What answers then do philosophers have to offer? As one would
expect, philosophers agree about this no more than scientists do. At
one time Catholic theologians claimed that *ensoulment* occurred at
the moment the fertilized egg became implanted in the uterine wall.
Few, if any, modern Catholic theologians would be that definite.[1]
The trend of thought would seem to be that since ensoulment occurs
at some unidentifiable stage it is better to err on the side of safety and
assume that it is at the earliest possible moment.

Essentially, the argument is whether it is the potential to develop
or actual possession of those attributes which constitute humanness
that determines that a being is human. If we follow the development

of the fetus in reverse, beginning with the point of birth, then it is difficult to identify in what way the essential nature of the fetus has changed at each stage. The fetus immediately pre-birth is exactly the same as that which emerges àt the time of birth. And so, we can backtrack through all the stages of fetal development. Nothing enters the fetus at any point to bring about the next development.

Take, for example, the commencement of electrical activity in the brain. This occurs naturally as part of the growth cycle. One cannot claim that because cessation of brain activity is synonymous with death that before brain activity begins there is no life, when clearly there is. 'The developing embryo has the natural capacity to bring on the functioning of the brain' (Varga 1980). For the brain to start functioning there must already be life present. It is not the brain but something else which provides the impetus.

Throughout development it is something already present which sparks off the change or the next stage. Thus we begin to see that there is something in the embryo itself which starts the development of all human activities. It seems logical therefore to take as the starting point of *human life* the time of conception, for that is the point at which two hitherto separate entities (i.e. the sperm and the ovum) come together to make a new entity which is potentially a newborn child. 'There comes a point where the personhood of the fetus is either an article of faith or it is not' (Campbell 1975). The argument that human life begins with fertilization may not be totally convincing and like most philosophical arguments it cannot be proven in the way that, for example, a law of physics can. 'Nevertheless, it has enough weight to establish at least the probability of the presence of a human individual at conception. This probability in turn substantiates the duty not to expose the developing fetus to danger or deliberately kill it, because we are obliged to choose the safer course and to avoid harming a being that is possibly or probably human' (Varga 1980).

The argument may appear very tortuous but we do need to try to establish the point at which human life begins before we can begin to discuss the ethics of abortion, research on embryos and other issues involving the unborn child. Clearly, if one were able with certainty to pin-point a stage in development at which human life began, say viability, then one could argue that there would be no need to afford to the unviable fetus the respect and rights we afford to a human being. The question of the morality of abortion pre-viability would possibly not arise. In the following pages the specific issues under discussion will be explored on the assumption that human life begins at conception.

Abortion

Having established the notion that the fetus is a human being we will now examine some of the arguments put forward to justify abortion. All the arguments are about comparing the *value* of the developing human life with some other value. In each case one has to decide which is the greater: the value of the life of the fetus or the conflicting value.

The 1967 Abortion Act gives the following as grounds for abortion:

1 That the continuance of the pregnancy would involve risk to the life of the pregnant woman or of injury to the physical or mental health of the pregnant woman, or of any existing children of her family, greater than if the pregnancy were terminated.
2 That there is a substantial risk that if the child were born it would suffer from such physical or mental abnormalities as to be seriously handicapped.

Therapeutic abortion

In cases where the mother's life is endangered then the choice which has to be made is between on the one hand destroying the life of the fetus and saving the life of the mother, and on the other allowing the pregnancy to continue and probably destroying the life of the mother. With advances in obstetrics, probably the only cases in which such a decision arises are those of ectopic pregnancies. In ectopic pregnancies, if the pregnancy is allowed to continue, the mother's life is clearly endangered. There is a strong likelihood that the fallopian tube will rupture and bleed. The embryo itself has no chance of survival anyway and so the choice is fairly clear-cut. Only the mother's life can be saved. It would clearly be unreasonable not to remove the embryo and let both lives perish.

If a situation arises, and today it is extremely rare, in which a choice has to be made between the life of the mother and the life of the unborn child, then one has to decide which life has the greater value. Campbell (1975) argues that 'It is difficult to see how the life of the fetus and the life of the mother can be regarded on an equal footing, far less that the fetus should be given priority'.

The main issue in *therapeutic abortion* is not deciding between one life and another but between the *life* of the fetus and the *health* of the pregnant woman. Advocates of therapeutic abortion would argue that the physical health of the pregnant woman is more valuable than the life of the fetus. Thus they would justify the act on the grounds that the greater value has been chosen. There are problems with this kind of justification. Firstly, as Varga (1980) argues, human life is more valuable than physical health and, secondly, there remains the question as to whether the abortion is necessary to restore health. Most complications of pregnancy can be dealt with by modern medicine. Illness arising during, but not caused by, pregnancy will not be cured by abortion and, whenever possible, if pregnancy intensifies the illness, remedies should be applied until the fetus reaches viability. There is no suggestion either that the health of the mother might not suffer as a result of the pregnancy or that physical health is not of high value. The argument is that the life of the fetus is of greater value than the physical health of the mother and that remedies other than abortion should be sought to improve the mother's health. The same basic argument, according to Varga, applies when the pregnancy affects the mental health of the mother.

What then of the contention in the Abortion Act 1967 that abortion is justified on the grounds that the continuance of the pregnancy would be harmful to any existing children? The argument here is based on the utilitarian principle of the greatest happiness for the greatest number. It can be argued that if as a result of the pregnancy and subsequent birth the health and well-being of existing children will suffer, then abortion is justified. The ending of the pregnancy will result in, if not benefit to, at least the prevention of harm to the other children. The arrival in a large family of an additional, perhaps unwanted, child will clearly have an effect on all concerned. The existing children may well suffer as a result of meagre resources having to be spread further and from a loss of attention from their mother. The new arrival might also have a less than ideal existence. The argument against abortion on such grounds is two-fold. Firstly, one can only conjecture the effect of the arrival of an additional child and, secondly, it is to equate the value of human happiness and well-being with the value of human life.

Before moving on to the second main reason given in the Abortion Act for justifying abortion – the risk that the unborn child will be severely handicapped – we will consider one other frequently posed justification.

Rape and incest

It is commonly argued that abortion is justified when the pregnancy occurs as a result of rape or incest. This is a very sensitive and emotive area, and in attempting to discuss objectively the morality of abortion in such situations, we must be careful not to appear insensitive to the very real sufferings of women who are victims of rape or incest.

It is argued that abortion under these circumstances is justified for three reasons: firstly, that abortion will safeguard the mental health of the woman, which is undoubtedly at risk and of great value; secondly, that pregnancy resulting from rape or incest is a grave injustice and that the victim is therefore under no obligation to carry the fetus to viability; and finally, it is sometimes argued that the fetus is an aggressor against the woman's personal life and integrity, and that it is morally defensible to repel an aggressor, even by killing him in order to protect human values.

The third argument carries less weight than the other two. The fetus is not the aggressor. It is the perpetrator of the rape who is the aggressor and the fetus is as much the innocent victim of the act as is the woman. The destruction of the fetus cannot be justified on this ground.

The strict objective moral argument against abortion in such cases on the grounds of the effects it will have on the mental well-being of the mother is that the value of human life 'has to be placed higher on the scale of values than the values a woman could obtain by abortion' (Varga 1980). However, society clearly has a moral duty toward rape victims and should offer to them far more in terms of psychological help and support than it frequently does. On humane grounds, unless there is adequate support, then abortion appears to be a reasonable solution. Sadly, the psychological effects of an abortion may well compound rather than alleviate those of the rape.

Eugenic abortion

Eugenic abortion is abortion of a fetus which if allowed to survive would result in a child with severe physical or mental handicap. The handicapping condition may, for example, be caused by viral infections such as exposure to rubella during the first trimester, the use of certain drugs during pregnancy (thalidomide was a tragic case in point), or due to genetic defects (Down's syndrome being one of the commonest). It is argued that it is better for a child not to be born than to lead a life burdened with a crippling disorder.

Modern medical advances, such as amniocentesis, have made it possible to identify an abnormal fetus at an early stage and therefore made possible abortion at a stage permitted in law. As our ability to identify more and more abnormalities at an increasingly early stage improves, so the question of abortion as a solution is more frequently raised. 'Some eugenicists would even made it obligatory to destroy seriously defective life before birth. As it stands now, eugenic abortion is legal in most countries but not obligatory' (Varga 1980). As has been argued elsewhere in this book, the ability to do something or the fact that an act is legal does not mean that it is morally right. What then is the morality of eugenic abortion?

It is argued that eugenic abortion is primarily for the benefit of the child and only secondarily for the benefit of the parents. This argument is a false one. The abortion is not for the benefit of the patient, who is the child. Abortion will not cure his disease but destroy him. It could of course be argued that ending the child's life before it has really begun is preventing a lift of suffering and misery and that it does benefit him. In so arguing, one is weighing the value of life itself against the value accorded to the quality of that life. Even if one claims that is a justifiable balancing of values, one still has the problem of measuring the unknown – the quality of a life which is as yet still developing. Just as we saw in Chapter 3 that it is very difficult to assess the quality of life of someone who cannot communicate their feelings, so it is impossible to assess the quality of life of an unborn child.

The other argument is that in preventing the birth of a severely handicapped child one is avoiding the hardships and suffering that caring for the child would place on the family, and the expense to society in meeting the child's and family's needs. Here, as in the case of therapeutic abortions, one is balancing two unequal values – the life of a human being against the suffering of others.

Against all of this we have the evidence that many children born with severe handicaps live enjoyable and worthwhile lives. Furthermore: 'Our social nature imposes a duty upon us and the whole society to look after the less fortunate members of the human family. That many persons understand this obligation of our common humanity is indicated by the fact that the number of couples adopting victims of genetic defects has been growing rapidly' (Varga 1980).

The rights of the woman

Many would argue that a woman has a right to abortion if, for whatever reason, she does not wish to bear the child. The main argument is based on the notion of the *right to privacy*. 'Respect for privacy is the basis for the concern that the pregnant woman maintain control over her own body' (Fenner 1980). If we accept the notion that, in other contexts, patients have the right to determine what shall be done to their bodies, then why should that notion not also apply to a pregnant woman? The argument would seem to be particularly strong with respect to the woman whose pregnancy is not of her choosing (see the Case for discussion at the end of this chapter).

Furthermore, in some circumstances, particularly when the pregnancy is the result of rape or incest, the quality of life of the mother may be severely harmed, and the quality of life of the 'unwanted' child may be minimal. Pro-abortionists would argue that *quality of life* is equally as important as *right to life*, and that by overvaluing life *per se* the quality of life comes into question.

In vitro fertilization

In vitro fertilization (IVF) is the process by which an ovum is removed from a woman's body, mixed with the sperm of her husband, and placed in a growth medium. Fertilization then occurs and after a period of 10–14 days the *blastocyst* (the eight cell stage) is implanted in the woman's uterus and, hopefully, the pregnancy proceeds as normal. The first child born as a result of IVF was Louise Brown in 1978[2] but that was only after years of experimentation.

The ethical debate surrounding IVF is wide ranging. One major concern is that of risk of damage to the embryo which could result in an abnormal baby. The risk is not thought to be great but there is still uncertainty about how great or slight it might be. The question of whether or not to take the risk has to be decided by the couple, but as Fromer (1981) points out, because of the lack of knowledge they are not able to make an *informed* decision; their decision will be a more or less blind one. The key question is whether the risk of damage is greater than that which occurs during the course of nature. In other words, is there a greater risk of danger occurring between IVF and implantation than there is between the time of natural fertilization and implantation? Some moral philosophers and scientists argue that even if the risk is only slightly increased, then it is morally unacceptable.

IVF also involves the question of rights. 'A barren couple has the right to take action and to use available technology to counteract that barrenness' (Fromer 1981). If IVF represents a couple's only possible hope of counteracting their barrenness then IVF comes to be seen as a *therapeutic* rather than an *experimental* procedure. Equally, the doctor has the right to give what he considers to be the most appropriate therapy to a barren couple as he has to any 'patient'. One could even claim that he has a duty so to do. Therefore, it is argued, the decision involves the couple and the doctor, and neither the State nor any other outside body has the right to interfere.

Then there is the question of what rights, if any, the blastocyst has. This takes us back to the earlier debate about when human life begins. If one takes the view that human life begins with implantation then clearly the blastocyst cannot be considered an entity and therefore has no rights. If on the other hand one takes the view that human life begins with fertilization, then the minute collection of cells which begins to form *in vitro* from the moment of fertilization must be treated with the respect due to a human being.

The concern of most moralists is not so much with the procedure of IVF itself but with some of the developments which could possibly arise from it. At the moment it is not possible to keep an embryo alive outside the uterus much beyond the blastocyst stage, still less bring it to full term. The fear of some moralists is that in time it will be possible that there will be such a thing as the artificial womb. Already scientists have laid claim to keeping an embryo alive for as much as 59 days (Varga 1980). The embryo has by this time reached a stage of development not normally achieved until after implantation. Is it human or not?

The possibility of growing babies in the laboratory is still very much in the future but IVF does make other developments possible in the here and now.

Surrogate mothers

In IVF the woman's ovum is removed, fertilized, and then implanted in her own uterus. The natural development of this procedure has been the transfer of an embryo. It is now possible for doctors to implant the ovum fertilized *in vitro* in the uterus of another woman or to transplant an embryo from the uterus of one woman to that of another. Women who carry an unborn child on behalf of another have come to be known as *surrogate mothers*.

Clearly this offers several *infertile* couples a tremendous sense of hope. The child, although carried by, and delivered of, a third party would genetically be theirs. 'One could argue that it respects human life and that it is only good medicine to help childless couples to have their own genetic children' (Varga 1980). Some ethicists of the natural law school would argue that this procedure is contrary to natural law, that it is an interference with natural biological processes. However, such an argument is rather weak inasmuch as a great deal of medical intervention is an interference with natural processes. To argue that interference in some instances is wrong and in others is right is clearly illogical.

Two issues which arise from the possibility of surrogate motherhood and which are of great concern to moralists are the use of the procedure for convenience rather than necessity, and payment of the surrogate mother.

Suppose an unmarried woman, who is committed to her career, wishes to raise a child. She does not however wish to interrupt her career by becoming pregnant. She could enlist the services of another woman to carry her child. The argument against such an idea revolves around the concept of motherhood. There is a distinction between the woman who desperately wants a child but for some medical reason is unable either to conceive or to carry a child to full term, and one who is quite able to do so but for reasons of convenience chooses not to. Some would question the woman's motives in having a child, for it might seem that the child is being brought into existence for purely selfish reasons and not for his or her own sake as a person, but this might equally well be said of children born naturally to some parents. We should not assume that because a woman elects not to carry her own child that she will not care for and value that child when it is born.

The idea of payment being made to surrogate mothers is abhorrent to many. It has long been established, since the abolition of slavery, that human beings are not a saleable commodity. It could, on the other hand, be argued that a couple were not *buying* the child from the surrogate mother, but simply paying her for nurturing it from the moment of implantation to the time of birth, and that there is no difference in that and paying a nanny or child-minder to care for the child after birth.

Of even greater concern to moralists is the notion of payment being made to a third party, such as an agent for surrogacy. To commercialize what is seen as being a humane service, and to make a profit out of the needs and sufferings of childless couples, is abhorrent to many. It is argued that, just as for adoption, the surrogacy arrangements should be made by the State or a voluntary organization who have at interest the needs of the parents and the child. The treatment of infertility can be viewed in the same way as the treatment of other health problems, and is something to which people have a right. The ability to exercise that right should not be determined by the ability to pay.

Donation of ovum

There is a further possible development of the principle of embryo transfer. Suppose a woman is unable to ovulate or to produce healthy ova. She could be helped in one of three ways. The ovum of another woman could be fertilized by her husband either by artificial insemination of the other woman or *in vitro*, and the fertilized ovum implanted in the *sterile* woman. Alternatively the ovum of another woman could be transferred to the sterile woman and then fertilized *in vivo* by her husband. The child, when born, would be the genetic child of only one partner, the husband, and a third party. The moral argument against such a procedure is that a third person is introduced into the marriage which is contrary to the notion that a marriage is by nature the exclusive relationship of one man and one woman. The same argument is used against artificial insemination by donor, not the husband.

Underlying the concerns about IVF and embryo transfer is the question of the safety of the procedure both to the child and the mother. Dr Steptoe is reported as saying that the birth of Louise Brown came only after 'roughly a hundred unsuccessful efforts' (Varga 1980). At present, embryo transfer involves the destruction of several embryos. If human life begins at the time of fertilization then such a practice is unethical because it involves the destruction of human life.

Experimentation on embryos

'It has been suggested that tampering with the embryo is itself unethical. This problem arises from the lack of agreement as to when human life begins' (Royal College of Nursing 1983). Is the embryo a human life or not? If it is, then should we afford to it the respect we afford to human persons in general? As we have already seen, the answer to the first of these questions is that we do not know for certain. The case for saying that human life does not begin until implantation is a strong one, but there are good reasons for arguing the contrary view. Whatever the case, where there is doubt then the safer course should be taken. A fertilized ovum has therefore to be treated with the respect that is due to a human life. 'One has to conclude that the bringing into existence and destruction of human embryos for the sake of experimentation is unethical' (Varga 1980).

Proponents of research on embryos argue that it is justifiable because it is undertaken for one of two main reasons; firstly, to perfect existing or develop new procedures for helping apparently infertile couples, and secondly, to discover ways of preventing congenital or hereditary disorders. They would argue that the benefits to be obtained from embryo research are sufficient to justify bringing embryos into existence for the purpose of research even if it results in the destruction of the embryo. However, if human life is present in the embryo, it is difficult to see how any benefits, however great, can justify the creation of embryos solely for the purposes of experimentation and with the almost total certainty of destruction.

Suppose that an embryo was brought into existence, not primarily for the purpose of research but with the intention that it should be implanted and allowed to develop naturally to birth. Suppose, too, that it was possible to carry out research on that embryo without endangering its life. If the embryo is a human life than research on it, given the conditions just described, can only be justified if it complies with the criteria pertaining to experimentation on human beings, i.e. that the experiment will not harm the subject and is designed to benefit him or her.[3] Benefit to others should only be a secondary outcome and not the prime reason for the research. In the case of most research carried out on embryos the main purpose is to benefit others, and there is a high risk of harm being done to the subject.

Summary

In all ethical issues relating to the unborn child the underlying question is 'When does human life begin?' As we have seen, it is difficult, if not impossible, to categorically state at what stage in its development the unborn child becomes a human person. It seems therefore prudent to err on the side of safety and assume that human life begins at the moment of fertilization. That being so, when discussing issues involving the unborn child, we must assume that we are dealing with a human life.

In this chapter some of the main arguments surrounding a few of the issues (abortion, *in vitro* fertilization, embryo transfer and research on embryos) have been discussed. There are other issues, e.g. artificial insemination, eugenics and genetic engineering, of which space does not permit discussion here. However, hopefully the reader has been provided with a framework on which to base discussion of these other issues.

The concern in this chapter has been with the ethics of the acts themselves. In Chapter 12 we shall discuss the rights of the nurse when asked to participate in procedures, such as abortion, which she might hold to be morally wrong, and her duties toward patients undergoing such procedures.

Case for discussion

Sarah Jones is 36 years old; she is married to Ted and they have five children whose ages range from 2 to 15 years. Sarah is pregnant. Ted, a bricklayer, has been unemployed for six months. He spends most of their small income on drink or gambling. Frequently he returns home late from the public house, drunk and aggressive. Often on these occasions he assaults Sarah, both verbally and physically.

For medical reasons the only contraceptive device they can safely use is the sheath, which Ted frequently 'forgets' to use, especially when under the influence of alcohol. Sarah's present pregnancy is the end result of one of Ted's drinking bouts, when, as he often does, he forced his attentions on her.

Despite their unkempt appearance the children are much loved by Sarah, who grieves over the departure of Tracey, the eldest. Tracey was taken into care three months ago after she had been sexually assaulted by Ted. Ted frequently hits the other children, but so far Sarah has managed to prevent him giving any of them a severe beating.

Sarah, who looks frail and exhausted, goes to her family doctor and asks for an abortion. She says she cannot cope with another child, and that she had neither wish nor intention of becoming pregnant in the first place – 'it was Ted's fault'. She is also afraid that this child, like her youngest, will be mentally handicapped.

Notes

1 See the Declaration on Procured Abortion: Sacra Congregatio pro Doctrina Fidei (1974), 'Declaratio di abortu procurato', *Acta Apostolicae Sedis*, pp. 730–747.
2 The birth of Louise Brown was the culmination of many years' experimentation by Dr Robert Edwards and Dr Patrick Steptoe. Previously, in 1959, Dr Daniele Petrucci, and Italian geneticist and biologist, claimed to have successfully fertilized a human ovum *in vitro* and kept the developing embryo alive for 29 days, after which he destroyed it because it had become deformed. In 1974, Dr Douglas Bevis of Leeds University, England, announced that he had successfully implanted human ova, fertilized in test tubes, in the wombs of three women who had given birth to healthy babies. Despite Dr Bevis' bona fide reputation as a researcher, scientists are unwilling to accept his claim because of the immense veil of secrecy he drew over the identity of the women and babies.
3 See Chapter 8 in which experimentation on human beings is discussed more fully.

References

Campbell, A.V. (1975), *Moral Dilemmas in Medicine*, Edinburgh: Churchill Living-stone.
Fenner, K.M. (1980), *Ethics and Law in Nursing: Professional Perspectives*, New York: Van Nostrand.
Fromer, M.J. (1981), *Ethical Issues in Health Care*, St. Louis: C.V. Mosby.
Royal College of Nursing (1983), The Unborn Generations – Humanity or Convenience?, *Nursing Mirror*, June 1, pp. 23–29.
Varga, A.C. (1980), *The Main Issues in Bioethics*, New York: Paulist Press.
Veatch, R.M. (1981), *A Theory of Medical Ethics*, New York: Basic Books.

Further reading

Foot, P. (1967), The Problem of Abortion and the Doctrine of the Double Effect, *Oxford Review*, Vol. 5, pp. 5–15.
Fromer, M.J. (1981), *Ethical Issues in Health Care*, St Louis: C.V. Mosby. See Chapters 3, 'Genetic manipulation'; 4, 'Overpopulation'; 5, 'Artificial insemination'; 7, 'Abortion'.
Iveson-Iveson, J. (1984), The Birth Revolution, *Nursing Mirror*, November 7, Vol. 159, No. 17.

Robinson, J. (1984), The Other Side of the Question, *Nursing Mirror*, May 16, Vol. 158, No. 20. Discusses the psychological effects on women as a result of much current opinion on the subject of abortions.

Royal College of Nursing (1983), The Unborn Generations – Humanity or Convenience?, *Nursing Mirror*, June 1, pp. 23–29. The RCN's evidence to the Warnock Committee.

Thompson, I.E., Melia, K.M. and Boyd, K.M. (1983), *Nursing Ethics*, Edinburgh: Churchill Livingstone. See pp. 88–93 on 'Termination of Pregnancy'.

Varga, A.C. (1980), *The Main Issues in Bioethics*, New York: Paulist Press. See Chapters 4, 'Eugenics and the Quality of Life'; 6, 'Anomalous Forms of Procreation'; 7, 'Gene-splicing, Genetic Engineering'.

Warnock, M. (1985), *A Question of Life: The Warnock Report*. The Report of the Committee of enquiry with two new chapters. London: Blackwell.

8

HOSPITALS SHOULD DO THE
PATIENT NO HARM*

In Chapter 5, attention was drawn to the vulnerability of patients. Their vulnerability may in part be caused by their state of health; they may be confused, frightened or too weak to question the decisions of professionals or to ask for an explanation of their condition and its treatment. Their vulnerability may be increased by the attitude of staff toward them and by environmental factors. It is very easy therefore for staff (nurses, doctors and others) to mistakenly assume that the patient does not want to know more and does not want the responsibility of making decisions. Yet worse, professionals may decide that the patient cannot possibly understand.

I am not here talking so much about telling the patient that he is dying or that he has a chronic debilitating disease which is going to result in a life of increasing dependency and discomfort; I am talking about less dramatic information such as why a particular X-ray or blood test has been requested, or how his medication will act, and so on.

By not offering the patient more information or the chance to be involved in the decision making process we are doing him an injustice. We are ceasing to treat him as a rational human being. We are reducing his dignity and taking away more independence than does his illness. We are causing him harm. True, it may not be a deliberate intention to cause harm – in fact the intention may be quite the opposite. It is sometimes argued that by telling the patient more about his disease and his treatment we might increase his anxiety and thus hinder his recovery. The reverse is probably true. Anxiety is more likely to be increased by uncertainty and relieved by information. Certainly research has shown that information reduces anxiety and that as a result the patient's experience of pain is also reduced (Hayward 1973). Thus by withholding information from patients we do them harm.

* Florence Nightingale, Notes on Hospitals 1859.   87

Maintaining the patient's autonomy and dignity

'During episodes of illness the autonomy of patients should be maintained throughout treatment . . . and the active participation of patients in their own treatment should be facilitated by means of open and sensitive communication' (Royal College of Nursing 1976).

Nurses very clearly share responsibility for all that is done to and for a patient whilst in the care of the Health Service. Such is the nature of modern health care that few if any treatments and their effects can be held to be the responsibility of one discipline. Most treatments prescribed by doctors involve one or more other professional groups. This is probably more the case in institutions than in the community where the administration of the treatment may frequently be undertaken by the patient or a relative. Even in the community, nurses and less frequently other professionals will carry out treatments prescribed by the doctor. It is no justification to claim that I must do something because another professional of my own or another discipline has requested that it be done. In carrying out the treatment I share in the responsibility with the prescriber.

This is true not only of specific therapies but also of the routines of institutions and organizational structures. It is very easy for institutional routines to become unnecessarily rigid and to cause a reduction of patients' independence and dignity. In hospitals and similar institutions it is easy for routines to govern all that happens, and even for a routine to become an end rather than a means, so that every decision and every act is undertaken to fit the routine. Patients have to be fitted into the institution and its routines rather than the institution bending to fit the patient. Patients are denied the opportunity of making even the most basic everyday decisions, such as when to get up, when to go to bed, when to eat and so on. The question nurses need to ask themselves is why the patient is being wakened or requested to go to bed at a particular time. Is it because it is necessary to his treatment and recovery? Or is it because that is the time that has been laid down for all patients? If the former is the case then there is no further debate. If it is the latter then there is considerable room for discussion. To deprive a person of the opportunity to make such basic decisions as these is to greatly increase his dependence and decrease his autonomy. It is also to treat him as a child and therefore to undermine his dignity.

In Chapter 5 I suggested that requiring that patients in hospital wear night-clothes had a detrimental effect on communications between them and staff. The wearing of night-clothes also restricts their freedom. While it might be socially acceptable for people to walk about the hospital building in their night-clothes or maybe even to venture into parts of the hospital grounds, it is most certainly not acceptable for them to leave the immediate environs of the hospital. Thus, a patient admitted for investigations or some form of treatment which does not require him to be constantly in bed or on the ward is made a prisoner. There may be no medical reason for him not going for a walk or perhaps visiting the local shop. It may actually be necessary for him to be physically on the ward only at certain fairly specified times. Not only is this a restriction of his freedom but it may be detrimental to his recovery. A patient who is being rehabilitated might be greatly helped by being 'allowed out'.

It is not only in institutions such as hospitals and nursing homes that this happens but also in other settings. The patient at home may enjoy more freedom than his counterpart in hospital inasmuch as he has control over the way in which he spends most of his day. Even so, the organizational structure of the community health service can restrict the patient's independence as much as a hospital. Because staff are employed to work between certain hours this may mean that patients have to get up and go to bed at restricted times and that they have to have a bath in the middle of Thursday afternoon rather than early on Monday morning. True, to some extent, some of these restrictions are unavoidable but we should at least be aware of the ways in which patients' routines are being disturbed and whenever possible try to be flexible and meet their needs.

Generally, rather than insisting that the patient comply with set times, community health workers often refuse to give the patient any idea as to what time of day they will call. The patient is forced to wait around for several hours, perhaps still in his night-clothes. He cannot go out and does not like to get on with any work in case the nurse calls. He may have to answer the door to tradesmen or entertain visitors while still in his night-clothes at a time of day when normally one would be fully clothed. Thus the patient's life-style may be restricted, and his dignity suffers.

It is one of the first rules of nursing which all the nurse trainees learn that at all times they must ensure the patient's privacy when carrying out nursing procedures. This means more than pulling the screens round the patient -- that merely allows him to be hidden from sight. To then ask him questions of a personal and private nature in a voice clearly audible throughout the ward is to totally negate the purpose of pulling the screens. Since it is the nurse or other health worker who decides when screens are required the patient may find himself with little or no privacy at times when he would choose it. Take the visit of his wife for example. The couple may wish to embrace, kiss or simply hold hands, but naturally feel embarrassed at doing so in front of strangers. It is difficult to carry on a normal conversation when you feel you are being watched or when others keep interrupting. Yet in very few hospitals are patients permitted, let alone encouraged, to pull the screens round when they have visitors.

It is all too easy, albeit unintentional, for nurses to restrict patients' independence and lower their dignity. To do either or both is to reduce their health prospects. 'In view of this, a fundamental aspect of the nurse's responsibility to the patient can be seen as the maintenance and restoration of personal autonomy' (Royal College of Nursing 1976). This obviously means that the nurse should involve the patient in the decision-making process and keep him fully informed about his nursing care and treatment. It also means that the nurse has a responsibility to question the practices of other health care professionals and the policies and functioning of the organizational structure if she feels they are harmful to the patient or patients. In this context what is harmful is not only the *doing* of harm but *failing* to do what is in the best interests of the patient.

Experimentation on patients

'Medicine is an experimental science by its nature. Primitive men and ancient healers, trying to treat diseases, must have acted on a trial-and-error basis until an accepted medical practice had developed with respect to the cure of certain illnesses. This history of human experimentation is as old as the history of medicine.'
Varga 1980

Much medical experimentation is carried out not on patients but on otherwise healthy persons. Generally (Nazi Germany hopefully was an exception), these people volunteer to be subjects of the experiments. Even this does raise some ethical issues.

Take for example the Cold Research Unit in England. In this Centre the researchers attempt to cause their volunteers to catch a cold in order ultimately to find a cure. 'No problem', you may say, 'the subjects have all volunteered, the disease which the experimenters are trying to induce is a minor, if very irritating, one. There is no great risk so how can there by any moral objection?' Some religious believers might make strong objection on the grounds that the body is a 'gift of God', a 'temple of the Holy Spirit' and that we have a duty to care for it and not abuse it. To deliberately set out to abuse the body by inducing infection is therefore wrong.

Veatch and Sollito (1973) list eleven cases of experiments which raise far more disturbing ethical questions. In several of these experiments involving large numbers of people volunteers were subjected to potentially harmful drugs – in one instance LSD was used – and were not fully informed of the possible long-lasting effects these drugs might have on them.

It was concern about medical experimentation and research that led the World Medical Assembly to draw up a set of guidelines known as the Declaration of Helsinki. This defines the parameters within which researchers may operate, and distinguishes between Non-therapeutic Biomedical Research Involving Human Subjects (Non-clinical Biomedical Research) and Medical Research Combined with Professional Care (Clinical Research). The former includes research on volunteer healthy persons and patients 'for whom the experimental design is not related to the patient's illness', while the latter involves patients for whom there is a relationship between the experiment and their illness. It is to this category of research that we now turn our attention.

To some extent, of course, any medical treatment is in the nature of an experiment. The patient reports with a set of signs and symptoms; the doctor makes a diagnosis and prescribes treatment. He can never be absolutely certain that the treatment will be successful. The dosage of a drug may need adjusting or it may be necessary to try another form of treatment. The process cannot be likened to the 'trial-and-error' of primitive man, for obviously the doctor bases his decisions on knowledge gleaned from the work of others and from his own experience. Nevertheless, there is always present an element of the experimental. It is important to acknowledge this before making statements about the rightness or wrongness of experimentation on patients.

Many authorities have traditionally distinguished between two types of experiment – *therapeutic* and *non-therapeutic*. Therapeutic experiments are those designed to benefit the subject, to find a cure for his disease or to alleviate his suffering. Non-therapeutic experiments are designed not to help the research subject directly but to benefit others suffering the same disease. It has been argued that the distinction is not always so clear-cut. Some experiments may benefit the subject even though designed initially to benefit others. For example, experiments carried out on a patient to discover the cause of his disease may initially have been designed as part of an on-going research programme aimed at eventually discovering the cause and then a possible cure. Suppose, by chance, the cause is discovered as a result of these particular experiments and its discovery makes it possible to immediately treat the disease; then the research subject unexpectedly benefits and the experiments could be said, at least retrospectively, to be therapeutic.

To await the outcome of the experiments before deciding their precise nature is of course inadequate. The judgement as to whether an experiment is therapeutic or non-therapeutic has to be based on the original intention. If the intention is to directly benefit the subject then the experiment is therapeutic. If the intention is not so, then the experiment is non-therapeutic.

Why, one might ask, is it necessary to make any distinction between types of experiments? Is not the real question about the morality of human experiments? Either it is right or it is wrong to carry out experiments on human subjects. If, for whatever reason, we conclude that it is wrong then we call into question virtually all medical practice. If we conclude that it is right then very soon we need to draw up some guidelines and determine some limits. Very soon we begin to ask questions about the purpose of the experiment and whom it will benefit. To draw a distinction on the basis of whom experiments will benefit is a useful one.

If the experiment is designed to benefit the subject then, having accepted that human experimentation is not intrinsically wrong, it is difficult to argue against it. Of course other questions do need to be asked about the nature of the experiment, the risks involved and so on but, as a general principle, it is probably acceptable. If, on the other hand, the experiment is designed to benefit others and not the subject then we are in a very different ball game. To argue that an experiment on a human is justified solely because it will benefit others is to leave the way open for all kinds of obviously immoral acts such as those described in Chapter 1.

We now have to begin to ask a whole range of questions. Will the subject be harmed in any way? Will it cause him pain, discomfort, loss of freedom, loss of dignity? Will it hasten the course of his disease? Is the procedure involved in the experiment unacceptable to the subject? If the answer is 'yes' to any one of these questions then the experiment cannot be justified, even though it is highly probable that many thousands will benefit. And it can only ever be *highly probable* – never absolutely certain. The reason that it is unjustified is that to do something deliberately which will cause harm to a patient is wrong.

The patient is there because he is ill; he needs help and care and he has placed his trust in the professionals. It is his expectation that they will do their best to help him and prevent him from unavoidable suffering. To do otherwise is to betray his trust. Obviously, you might say, it is wrong to carry out such an experiment without telling the patient. What if the patient consents to the experiment? Would it not then be possible to justify it? To answer this question let us eavesdrop on a conversation between doctor and patient.

Dr Jones: Now, as you know, Mr Brown, we are not absolutely certain as to what causes your disease and until we do know we won't know how to cure it.

Mr Brown: Yes, Doctor.

Dr Jones: We think we are very close to finding the cause. In order to do this we need to do a few tests on one or two people who have the disease.

Mr Brown: I see . . . .

Dr Jones: They're really quite simple tests. It would mean staying here in hospital for a few more days, and then you would be able to go home.

Mr Brown: You want to do the tests on me?

Dr Jones: Yes, you see you have reached just the right stage of the disease.

Mr Brown: And you think that these tests will tell you what you need to know?

Dr Jones: Almost definitely, Mr Brown. Just think what it might mean, a cure for your disease. So many people will be helped.

Mr Brown: Well, of course, put like that I don't really have any choice do I?

Dr Jones: Thank you, Mr Brown, so if you would just sign this consent form. It's just the routine one, like the one you signed before you had your operation.

And so Mr Brown signs the form.

What has happened here? Mr Brown has been subjected to moral blackmail – 'I don't really have any choice'. It is significant that Dr Jones did not respond to that last question. He did not tell Mr Brown that he does indeed have a choice but by treating it as a rhetorical question, implying compliance, reinforces the notion that Mr Brown has no choice. Nor has the doctor told Mr Brown what the nature of these tests is, what they will entail and whether they will cause him pain, discomfort or distress. Mr Brown has not asked but that does not absolve the doctor from the responsibility to inform him. Furthermore, it has never been clearly established that if the cause is discovered the cure will be found in time to benefit Mr Brown.

If we are to be able to claim that experiments on an individual for the benefit to others are justified if that person consents to them, then his consent has to be freely given and fully informed. In the hypothetical conversation between Dr Jones and Mr Brown it could not be claimed that the consent was freely given nor was it fully informed.

'In any research on human beings, each potential subject must be adequately informed of the aims, methods, anticipated benefits and potential hazards of the study and the discomfort it may entail. He or she should be informed that he or she is at liberty to abstain from participation in the study and that he or she is free to withdraw his or her consent to participation at any time. The doctor should then obtain the subject's freely given informed consent, preferably in writing.'
Declaration of Helsinki 1975

Informed consent

The need for *informed consent* does not apply only to experimentation but to all medical and nursing procedures performed on a patient. 'Every human being of adult years and sound mind has a right to determine what shall be done with his own body; and a surgeon who performs an operation without his patient's consent commits an assault, for which he is liable in damages' (B.N. Cardoza 1914).

The notion that patients have a right to give or withhold consent to treatment, and that in order to make such a decision they have the right to sufficient information, is historically a recent one. One of the underlying reasons is that it will benefit the patient. It has been argued that in some cases getting sufficient information in order to give informed consent may not, on balance, benefit the patient. 'Traditionally the Hippocratic physician, in a case like this, who is interested in doing what he thinks will be for the benefit of the patient would apply the doctrine of "therapeutic privilege" ' (Veatch 1981). He would argue that the patient's consent should not be obtained for the patient's own good. Twentieth century society has clearly rejected this idea as evidenced by judgements made in the courts and laws passed by governments.

Having accepted the idea that patients have a right to informed consent there remain two vital questions. Firstly, what exactly do we understand by informed consent, and, secondly, what of those who are unable to give informed consent?

There is a danger that the giving of information by the professional in order to obtain the patient's consent may become a ritualized formality. The doctor or nurse could claim to have carried out their duty to give the information if they have provided that information in the language they understand. In other words, the patient has *received* the 'information' and can therefore be expected to give consent. Obviously if the process of obtaining informed consent is to be honest and meaningful then the patient has to be able to *understand* the information. There is a clear distinction between *informed consent* and *educated consent*.

The information has to be given to the patient in language he can understand and in sufficient detail for him to be able to make an educated decision. 'If a complication arises after the procedure, patients can deny, and have denied, that they understood what they were signing . . . . The law says you cannot sign away your rights in advance of a procedure and the courts have upheld awards in the face of signed Informed Consents. You may still be sued' (Demy 1971).

What then of those patients who are not capable of giving informed consent? 'We still have patients with language problems, the uneducated and the intelligent, the stolid and the stunned who cannot form an Informed Opinion to give an Informed Consent; we have the belligerent and the panicky who do not listen or comprehend' (Demy 1971). This statement of Demy's has strong paternalistic overtones. The types of patients he cites as being unable to form an informed opinion are probably quite capable of doing so given the information in an appropriate way and time to assimilate it.

Who really has the language problem – the patient or the professional? Just because someone does not understand or cannot communicate in our language does not mean *they* have a problem. The problem is ours and we have to find a way to communicate with them. If the patient is 'uneducated' then the professional has a responsibility to educate. To label someone 'unintelligent' is in many instances to make a subjective judgement based on opinion rather than objective facts. The person may be capable of understanding far more than we give them credit and the onus is on us to provide the information in a way that they can understand. The 'belligerent' and 'panicky' need time, patience and reassurance. Given more information they may become less belligerent and less panicky.

There are, however, some categories of patients who are genuinely incapable of forming an informed opinion. Perhaps the most obvious is the unconscious patient who requires life-saving surgery. Here, someone other than the patient has to make the decision on behalf of the patient. It may be possible to obtain consent from the patient's relatives but, if they are not available or the situation is an emergency and there is no time for lengthy explanations, then the surgeon is justified in making the decision to operate on the grounds that it is in the best interests of the patient.

A second group of patients from whom it may not be possible to obtain informed consent are children. Here, the usual and quite natural recourse is to obtain the parents' consent. Even so, there is a need for caution. While, obviously, a six-month-old baby is incapable of making a decision, a seven-year-old child is certainly capable of understanding what is happening to him. In law he may not have the authority to give or withhold his consent – that may rest with his parents. Nevertheless, morally he at least has a right to know and to be helped to understand what is happening to him. It seems to me that the professional, whether doctor or nurse, has here a two-fold moral duty. They have a duty to give the child as full an explanation of his treatment as he can reasonably be expected to understand. They also have a duty to prevent the parents, however well motivated, from making their decision without involving the child.

The third group is patients suffering severe mental handicap or brain damage. There have been several instances in which the nature of research carried out on severely mentally handicapped persons has been brought into question, not least those in Nazi Germany. If one starts from the premise that mentally handicapped people are humans and therefore have all the rights that others have by virtue of being human, then it becomes possible to draw up a set of moral guidelines. The two main principles must be (a) to give them the respect due to any human being and (b) to ensure that they are protected from harm.

It then becomes almost impossible to justify any form of experimentation on a mentally handicapped person other than that which will directly benefit that individual. It means that the professional has to examine very closely and honestly his reasons for giving any form of treatment. It does not make the decision making easy for the professional – indeed it makes it much more difficult. Consider the question as to whether young mentally handicapped women should be sterilized.

One side of the argument is that to sterilize such a woman is to deny her the right to childbirth which is a natural right of all women. On the other hand, she might be genuinely incapable of coping with childbirth and subsequently caring for a child, so to allow her to retain her reproductive capacity might be harmful. To argue that she should not be sterilized, on the grounds that she is incapable of giving informed consent to the operation, is to disregard the fact that she is equally incapable of informedly withholding consent. In protecting her right to childbirth one would be denying her right to reliable, uncomplicated control over reproduction. The woman's parents, legal guardians or physician have to make the decision on her behalf. It has to be made on the basis of the evidence in each individual case. Which course of action will benefit or cause the least harm to the patient? It is not possible to make generalized rules, such as all mentally handicapped females with an IQ of 50 or below should be sterilized.

The right to refuse treatment

It follows that if patients have the right to informed consent then they have the right to withhold consent. If, having been given sufficient information and having understood what they have been told, they decide not to undergo the treatment, then that is their right.

'Health professionals are not used to having their services refused and are usually shocked when it happens' (Fromer 1981). One reason for this reaction may be because health professionals, and nurses in particular, work in a hierarchical structure. They are used to receiving and carrying out instructions from above and to giving instructions to, and having them carried out by, those below them.

There is also a strong feeling of knowing what is best for the patient who it is thought cannot possibly have as much knowledge as the professional. The refusal to consent to treatment is often viewed as a criticism of the professional's competence.

If patients refuse treatment then this must be seen as a function of their autonomy and health professionals have a responsibility to find out the reason for refusal. The patient's decision may be based on accurate information and rationality or it may be based on inaccurate information and emotion. If the former then the professional should respect that decision but, if the latter, the professional has a responsibility to provide more accurate information. It is vital too to give the patient unlimited opportunity to change his mind. The consent form, once signed, is not binding. The patient can request that it be torn up.

The situation may become complicated when the patient is considered mentally unbalanced. Here it may be justifiable to claim that the patient, albeit temporarily, is incapable of making a rational decision to either consent to or to refuse treatment. The professional is then justified in deciding in the best interests of the patient whether or not the treatment should be given. In practice what frequently happens is that the patient is asked first if he will voluntarily assent to treatment. If he does so then the professional feels justified in going ahead. If the patient refuses, the professional may then judge him to be incompetent and feel justified in giving the treatment without consent. The professional thereby lays himself or herself open to the criticism that voluntary compliance indicates rationality while refusal indicates incompetence. To put it simply: 'If you agree with me you are rational, if you disagree you are not'. The judgement about a patient's competence to choose must be made before giving him the choice.

Summary

In this chapter we have considered some of the ways in which patients' vulnerability may put them at risk of being harmed. Some of the issues considered, such as freedom of choice about getting up, when to eat, what to wear, seem rather undramatic when compared with the issues raised by experimentation and informed consent. They may be less dramatic in their effects but the moral principles involved are equally important. We are concerned throughout with basic human rights and freedom.

There is no great difference in principle between denying the patient the right to decide what to wear and the right to decide whether to undergo treatment. To deny either is to restrict his autonomy. Paternalism means controlling the activities of another, and a health professional may justify a paternalistic action on the grounds that it will benefit the patient. Autonomy and paternalism frequently conflict, especially in the matter of informed consent, and when they do dilemmas arise.

> Paternalism may be justified, usually when the client's safety is in jeopardy and paternalistic action will prevent harm, but these instances are few and far between. Careful deliberation is necessary before paternalism in informed consent can be justified. Restricting liberty is almost never morally permissible.
> *Fromer 1981.*

References

Cardoza, B.N. (1914), 'Schloendorff v New York Hospital'. In Gorovitz, S. et al (eds) (1976), *Moral Problems in Medicine*, Englewood Cliffs, N.J.: Prentice-Hall.

Declaration of Helsinki, adopted by the 18th World Medical Assembly in 1964 in Helsinki and revised by the 29th World Medical Assembly in Tokyo, 1975.

Demy, N.J. (1971), 'Informed Opinion on Informed Consent'. In Gorovitz, S. et al (eds) (1976), *Moral Problems in Medicine*, Englewood Cliffs, N.J.: Prentice-Hall.

Fromer, M.J. (1981), *Ethical Issues in Health Care*, St. Louis: C.V. Mosby.

Hayward, J. (1973), *Information – A Prescription Against Pain*, London: RCN.

Royal College of Nursing (1976), *RCN Code of Professional Conduct – a Discussion Document*, London: RCN.

Veatch, R.M. (1981), *A Theory of Medical Ethics*, New York: Basic Books.

Veatch, R.M. and Sollito, S. (1973), *Human Experimentations – The Ethical Questions Persist*, Hastings Centre Report, cited in Varga, A.C. (1980), *The Main Issues in Bioethics*, New York: Paulist Press.

Varga, A.C. (1980), *The Main Issues in Bioethics*, New York: Paulist Press.

Further reading

Besch, L.B. (1979), Informed Consent: A Patient's Right, *Nursing Outlook*, January 1979, Vol. 27, Part 1, pp.32–35.

Freedman, B. (1975), *A Moral Theory of Informed Consent*, Hastings Centre Report, August 1975, Vol. 5, Part 4, pp.32–39.

Gorovitz, S. et al (eds) (1976), *Moral Problems in Medicine*, Englewood Cliffs, N.J.: Prentice-Hall. See collections of papers on 'Informed Consent and Coercion' and 'Paternalism'.

Murchison, I. et al (1978), *Legal Accountability in the Nursing Process*, St. Louis: C.V. Mosby.

Ramsey, P. (1970), *The Patient as a Person*, New Haven: Yale University Press.

Thompson, I.E., Melia, K.M. and Boyd, K.M. (1983), *Nursing Ethics*, Edinburgh: Churchill Livingstone. See in particular Chapter 4 on 'Moral Dilemmas in direct nurse/patient relationships'.

9

CONFIDENTIALITY

Most, if not all, codes of nursing ethics include statements about confidentiality, though none claim that all that passes between patient and nurse shall in all circumstances be regarded as confidential. There seems to be debate as to what information can be regarded as confidential, and whether in certain circumstances confidential information can or should be divulged. We shall explore these issues later, but first we must consider why the notion of confidentiality figures so frequently in nursing codes of ethics.

The nurse–patient relationship

The relationship between nurse and patient, as between doctor and patient, is *special*. 'Special relationships are those in which particular duties and obligations are owed and in which certain duties and obligations go beyond the scope of ordinary social intercourse' (Fromer 1981). That in the nurse–patient relationship 'particular duties and obligations are owed' is a generally accepted idea. Nursing codes set out the duties of nurses toward patients and certainly some of these are beyond the scope or ordinary social intercourse.

What then are the elements of the nurse–patient relationship which make it special? Perhaps the most essential element is that if it is to be effective it must be built on trust. The nurse needs to know that the patient has trust in her, that he trusts her professional judgement and that he trusts in her knowledge and skills. At the same time the nurse has to be able to have trust in the patient, to trust that he will tell her all that she needs to know in order to give him the most appropriate nursing care.

The information about himself which the patient gives to the nurse to enable her to make professional judgements is information which he would not divulge in the course of normal social interaction. This then is a second element in the nurse–patient relationship which makes it special and which is pertinent to the notion of confidentiality. Furthermore, the nurse is privy to information about the patient of a private or confidential nature which she obtains from sources other than the patient himself. The nurse may receive information from the patient's relatives or from his medical records.

The nurse then knows a lot about the patient, which may be known only to herself, the patient and at most one or two others. She obtains that knowledge solely because he is the patient and she is the nurse and needs it to give care. The knowledge is therefore privileged. This then confers on the nurse a duty to keep such information confidential and gives to the patient the right to expect that she will do so. Confidentiality is an integral component of the nurse–patient, or indeed any health professional–client, relationship.

> The nurse–client relationship is built on trust. This relationship could be destroyed and the client's welfare and reputation jeopardized by injudicious disclosure of information provided in confidence.
> *American Nurses' Association, 1976.*

What information?

As mentioned earlier, all the major codes of nursing ethics contain a statement about confidentiality. The 1973 Code for Nurses of the International Council of Nurses states that 'The Nurse holds in confidence personal information'. The 1976 American Nurses' Association Code for Nurses states 'The nurse safeguards the client's right to privacy by judiciously protecting information of a confidential nature' and the 1984 UKCC Code of Professional Conduct for the Nurse, Midwife and Health Visitor holds that 'Each registered nurse, midwife and health visitor . . . shall respect confidential information obtained in the course of professional practice and refrain from disclosing such information without the consent of the patient/client.' It seems implicit in all three of these statements that not all information which the nurse gains is to be held in confidence, that not all the patient tells the nurse is told in confidence, nor is it of a confidential nature.

Some information is clearly confidential such as information which relates specifically to the patient's condition and nursing care. The patient has every right to expect that the nurse will not pass such information to the patient in the next bed, nor to all the passengers on her bus going home. It may be, of course, essential for the patient's well-being that she pass the information on to a senior nurse or a doctor, in which case she should tell the patient so. For example, suppose a patient tells a junior nurse that he has been constipated for three days or that he has a severe headache. If the nurse is going to be able to help the patient with these problems, she has got to pass the information to someone with the authority to prescribe the appropriate treatment. Thus, in some instances information which is of a personal nature may be divulged by the patient to one professional on the understanding that it remains confidential to himself, the first professional and those other professionals who need that information.

It is not only information which the patient gives the professional that is confidential, but also information given by the professional to the patient. The patient has the right to expect that his diagnosis, for example, is confidential information. He does not expect that the doctor or nurse will give that information to other patients or the world in general. All information which might be described as 'clinical' is clearly of a confidential nature – the patient's symptoms, diagnosis, treatment and prognosis.

However, some information is clearly not of a confidential nature. Patients will tell nurses things about themselves which they do not expect to be held in confidence, things which would form part of normal social intercourse. Suppose, for example, patient A tells a nurse that he went to Majorca for holiday last summer, and later in the day patient B tells the same nurse that he is thinking of going to Majorca for his holiday but is not sure if he will like it. Obviously there is no reason why the nurse should not tell patient B that patient A has been there and suggest they get together. To put patients with like interests in touch with one another may well be beneficial to their general well-being and recovery.

Between these two ends of the scale, clinical information and social chit-chat, lie many less clear areas. If a patient 'confides' in a nurse about something in his personal life which is causing him anxiety then the nurse may face something of a dilemma. Firstly, she has to be able to decide whether this information is being told her in confidence. If the patient says that it is, that he does not want her to tell anyone else, and she agrees to treat it so, then she has placed on herself a moral obligation to keep that information confidential. Of course the patient may not say that he wants the information to be treated as confidential until after he has divulged it. This may make the decision more difficult for the nurse. Then again the patient may not verbalize his wish that the information be treated confidentially but may imply it by his tone of voice or other non-verbal cues. The nurse may need to ascertain from the patient just what his wishes are in the matter.

What if, for example, the nurse considers that it would be beneficial to the.patient for the information to be passed to another member of the health care team, and for it to be detrimental to the patient's recovery for it not to be? In such a situation the nurse has two possible lines of action: either she can explain that it is important that she pass the information on and why, and ask the patient's permission to do so, or she can strongly recommend that the patient himself tell the senior nurse, doctor, or whoever. If the patient refuses either of these options does the nurse have a moral duty to keep the confidence?

The response of many readers to that question will probably be, 'It depends'. Depends on what? It depends perhaps on a number of factors: the nature of the information, the extent to which it or the anxiety it is causing may have an effect on the patient's recovery, the patient's diagnosis and prognosis, and so on. I have deliberately refrained from using a specific example because what I am trying to do is to establish a principle. Can we say as a matter of principle that (a) patients have a right to confidentiality, and (b) nurses have a duty to uphold that right?

The question we first have to consider is whether the patient's right to confidentiality is an absolute right. If it is, then the nurse is bound to uphold it. If it is not, then the next question is how binding is the duty of the nurse to keep confidences?

'The patient has the right to expect that all communications and records pertaining to his care should be treated as confidential' (American Hospital Association 1972). It seems implicit in that statement and the one which precedes it in the Patients' Bill of Rights that there is no expectation that the information is confidential between the patient and one profesisonal but between the patient and several professionals. The preceding statement includes, for example, a reference to case conferences. This supports the suggestion earlier in this chapter that health carers have a right to share information about patients in their care. The patient cannot expect one clinician to keep vital information from another involved in his care.

If, for example, a district nurse were to request that a specialist nurse visit a patient to advise on the care of that patient, it would be unreasonable for the patient to expect the nurse not to give some sort of report to the district nurse, in just the same way as a doctor may call in a specialist colleague for a second opinion. In such situations it can be argued that the patient has consented to the sharing of information between two professionals by consenting to see the specialist.

Are there circumstances in which a nurse might be justified in passing confidential information to another without the patient's permission? To answer this question we can refer back to the discussion in Chapter 5 about keeping promises. There we saw that while it might be generally agreed that one has a duty to keep a promise, one could be justified in breaking a promise in order to comply with a higher duty. The same principle applies here. The nurse is justified in breaking a confidence in order to comply with a higher duty such as the duty to preserve life.

So far we have established two principles. Firstly, that clinical information is of a confidential nature, but may be legitimately shared by members of the health team involved in the patient's care. Secondly, that information, although not strictly clinical, which has a bearing on the patient's progress or recovery may be treated in the same way as clinical information. We now turn to the question of whether members of the health team are ever justified in divulging confidential information to others.

One instance in which clinical information may be divulged is when the law or regulations require it. For example, in the United Kingdom there is a fairly extensive list of notifiable diseases. In such cases the health professional has a duty to divulge the information to the appropriate authority. Beyond this it is much more difficult to make definitive statements.

> Anyone who thinks that disclosure of confidential information is morally justified or even mandatory in some circumstances bears a burden of proof. While this approach requires a balancing of conflicting duties, it also establishes a structure of moral reasoning and justification.
> *Beauchamp and Childress 1979*

In other words, one starts from the presumption that confidences should not be revealed and has to produce a strong reasoned case for going against that presumption. This is important because it means in practice that one's first thought is to maintain confidentiality and only in exceptional circumstances is one prepared to break it. This therefore serves to safeguard the patient's interests and to maintain trust.

Let us consider three quite different cases involving the question of whether or not to break a confidence.

Case 1

A married man comes to see his general practitioner. He has previously been to the Special Clinic and knows he has contracted non-gonococcal urethritis. He is worried that he may have passed the disease to his wife, but does not want her to know that he has the disease nor how he caught it. He has therefore told the venereologist that he will ask his wife to see their general practitioner rather than visit the Special Clinic. He explains this to the general practitioner and asks him to send a card to his wife requesting that she attend for a routine examination. The doctor, although unhappy about this, eventually agrees because he is concerned that if the wife is infected she should have treatment.

Subsequently the wife calls at the surgery in response to a request that she attend for a routine examination. On examination she is found to have the disease. The doctor gives her a prescription telling her that she has a mild infection which will quickly clear up with a course of antibiotics.

Suppose the wife at this point asks to know what the infection is. The doctor would obviously feel obliged to tell her. Her next question is almost certain to be 'How did I catch it?' If the doctor tells her then he will be divulging confidential information about another patient, information which, in this case, the patient has clearly indicated he does not want to be divulged. Not to tell the wife would be to deceive her and to deny her her right to know. How can the doctor resolve this dilemma?

One way of approaching the problem is to pose the question 'Whose information is it?' In this particular case both husband and wife are patients with the same doctor. The doctor has the same duties toward each of them as he does to all his patients. They each have the same rights. The information, that is the diagnosis and its cause, belongs as much to the wife as to the husband. Since she has the disease the wife has as much right to know as has any patient to know his or her diagnosis. While the husband might lay claim to a right to confidentiality, he can only reasonably do so when the information is his alone, or when the exercising of that right does not impinge on the rights of another. Thus in this case the doctor would be justified in divulging confidential information, at least by implication, about one patient to another. The doctor does not have to tell the wife that her husband has the disease, nor, should she ask, how her husband caught it; that information she will quickly deduce for herself.

Of course, the doctor should have made absolutely clear to the husband that, in the event of his wife being found to have the disease, should she ask what was wrong with her she would have to be told. One could well claim that regardless of whether she asked for her diagnosis she should be told it – not to inform her of her husband's infidelity, but to prevent her from passing the disease to others.

In certain circumstances doctors and nurses are absolved from keeping clinical information confidential. One example, which has already been mentioned, is where the disease is notifiable. They are morally justified in doing so when required by law or health regulations to disclose information in the interest of public health and safety. 'In addition, it can be argued that such acts of disclosure do not involve a breach of confidentiality because, insofar as the relevant laws are public and knowable in advance, the health care provider does not obtain the information in question under the supposition that it will be held in confidence' (Benjamin and Curtis 1981).

In the case we have been considering it could be argued that the doctor was justified in divulging the information to the wife about her husband because it is a well-established practice to trace and offer treatment to all sexual contacts of a person with venereal disease.

Case 2

Sister Smith is employed as an occupational health nurse by a large engineering firm. One morning, Mr Jones, a fairly senior manager, comes into the surgery. He says that he has been suffering from headaches and dizzy spells on and off for the past two months. On being asked why he has waited until now to seek help, Mr Jones replied that this morning he had 'one of these spells and nearly blacked out'. This had frightened him and so he had come to the surgery.

Sister Smith asks him several questions about his headaches and dizzy spells, his general health and life-style. During their conversation she makes notes on Mr Jones's medical records. She then takes and records his pulse rate and blood pressure reading. His blood pressure is higher than when it was last recorded during a routine annual medical six months previously. It is also high enough for Sister Smith to be concerned and she strongly advises Mr Jones to see either his own general practitioner or the firm's visiting medical officer as soon as possible as she thinks he should have treatment. She arranges for Mr Jones to come back to the surgery in two weeks to have his blood pressure checked. ›

Shortly after Mr Jones has left the surgery, the personnel officer comes in. He knows that Mr Jones has been to the surgery and wants to know why. Sister Smith says she cannot tell him. The personnel officer goes on to explain that the Board will be meeting that afternoon and will be considering offering Mr Jones promotion. What he needs to know is whether Mr Jones is fit enough to undertake a more demanding job.

An initial response to this situation might be to say that the personnel officer has no right to be discussing a senior manager's promotion prospects with the nurse. However, the fact remains that he has, and Sister Smith has to decide how to respond.

What are Sister Smith's options? She could refuse to give any information on the grounds that it was confidential. She could suggest that the correct procedure would be for the Board to require that Mr Jones have a medical examination. She could tell the personnel officer part or all of the truth about Mr Jones's condition.

If she refuses to give any information, neither confirming nor denying that Mr Jones is perfectly fit, then she might in the long run not be acting in the best interests of her patient, for if he were to get the job, the additional stress of his new post might exacerbate his condition. Therefore, she might feel justified in disclosing at least some information about Mr Jones's state of health in his own interests. The compromise option of suggesting that the Board require Mr Jones to have a medical examination is probably the best solution here, particularly if such a course of action is a fairly normal procedure when selecting staff for promotion.

The divulging of confidential information in the interests of the client's own health or safety is generally accepted as being justifiable. In cases of non-accidental injury, for example, there is little or no doubt that the health professional has a moral as well as a legal duty to divulge relevant information. In the case under discussion the circumstances are perhaps less dramatic than non-accidental injury, and the nurses' responsibility less clear-cut. In cases of non-accidental injury the health worker has a duty to report relevant information to the appropriate authority. What is Sister Smith's duty? Does she have a duty to uphold her patient's right to confidentiality? Does she have a duty to act always in her patient's best interests? Clearly she does, as do all nurses, and there will be times when, as in the case under discussion, these two duties conflict. What Sister Smith has to decide is which is the superior duty.

Case 3

During the course of visiting a patient to give nursing care a district nurse notices that some items of new electrical equipment keep appearing and disappearing from the house. After a while she realizes there is a similarity between this equipment and reports in the local paper of items stolen in the area. When she casually remarks about the equipment to the patient, the patient laughingly replies that it's her son's business. 'He buys and sells – you know, it falls off the backs of lorries!'

The nature of the information here is obviously non-clinical. It could be claimed that it is within the bounds of normal social intercourse and therefore not confidential. On the other hand the nurse is privy to the information as a result of her privileged relationship with the patient. She is in the patient's home solely for professional reasons and as a guest in that home. If she reports her suspicions to the police she might destroy the relationship of trust between herself and the patient. The patient might refuse her entry in future and this could be detrimental to the patient's recovery.

There is no doubt as to her legal responsibility here. If she fails to report her suspicions to the police she could be guilty of withholding information about a criminal offence and possibly be liable to prosecution as an accessory after the fact. The nurse has the same duty as any other citizen to report a criminal offence. Probably the best course of action would be for the nurse to seek legal advice from a solicitor.

Summary

The question of confidentiality is extremely complex, and while the notion of confidentiality is an essential component of the nurse–patient relationship, it is not always easy to decide how far the nurse's duty extends. As we have seen there are some situations where the information can be clearly classified as confidential while in others the nurse may be justified in breaking a confidence in order to comply with a superior duty. Certainly some of the most frequently occurring dilemmas faced by nurses are those involving the question of confidentiality. It is perhaps not surprising therefore that codes of nursing ethics contain only rather generalized statements and not hard-and-fast rules. In law, at least in the United Kingdom, the nurse–patient is not privileged as are the lawyer–client or priest–penitent relationships, and nurses can be required in a court of law to divulge information of even the most confidential nature. It is of course still possible for a nurse to refuse to give the information on moral grounds and face the legal consequences of so doing. We shall return to the relationship between legal and moral duties in Chapter 12.

References

American Hospital Association (1972), *A Patients' Bill of Rights*, paragraph 6, American Hospital Association.

American Nurses' Association (1976), *Code for Nurses with Interpretive Statements*.

Beauchamp, T.L. and Childress, J.F. (1979), *Principles of Biomedical Ethics*, New York: Oxford University Press.

Benjamin, M. and Curtis, J. (1981), *Ethics in Nursing*, New York: Oxford University Press.

Fromer, M.J. (1981), *Ethical Issues in Health Care*, St. Louis: C.V. Mosby.

International Council of Nurses (1973), *Code for Nurses*, Geneva: ICN.

UKCC (United Kingdom Central Council for Nursing, Midwifery and Health Visiting) (1984), *Code of Professional Conduct for the Nurse, Midwife and Health Visitor*, London: UKCC.

Further reading

Gorovitz, S. et al (eds) (1976), *Moral Problems in Medicine*, Englewood Cliffs, N.J.: Prentice-Hall. See: 'Rights of Privacy in Medical Practice', Cass L.J. and Curran W.J.; 'Confidentiality and Privileged Communication', Chayet N.L.; 'Role of Physician and Breach of Confidence', Davidson H.A.

Reich, W.T. (ed) (1980), *Encyclopedia of Bioethics*, New York: Random House. See especially 'Confidentiality', Winslade W.J.

Veatch, R.M. (1981), *A Theory of Medical Ethics*, New York: Basic Books. See in particular Chapters 6 and 7.

10

TO TELL OR NOT TO TELL

In Chapter 8 we established that the patient has a right to *informed consent* and that if he was to be able to exert this right he required sufficient information. Patients cannot make a well-informed decision about whether or not to consent to treatment unless they are told the truth about their illness, its treatment and the consequences of that treatment. In this chapter our concern is with *truth telling*; whether doctors and nurses have a duty to tell the truth, or whether there are situations where the truth may be withheld. In cases of terminal illness to whom should the truth be told, when, and by whom? These are questions which are frequently raised by nurses and health workers and these are the questions with which this chapter is concerned.

What is truth?

Before we can begin to answer the questions posed above we need to establish what we mean by *truth* and *honesty*. Truth and honesty are not the same although the two concepts are closely related. Truth can be defined as 'the state of being the case: fact' (*Webster's Dictionary*), while honesty is 'fairness and straightforwardness of conduct or adherence to the facts'. Honesty then is a dynamic concept; it is about being truthful and is based on one's 'sincere and objective attempt to appraise a total situation and that is limited by his inability to be totally unbiased' (Salzman 1973). Truth, on the other hand, is determined by the framework within which it is established. It may be scientific truth, as defined by natural laws or factual measurement, or it may be moral truth as determined by God or man. 'Truth is largely defined by how you find it' (Oppenheimer 1955). In other words, what is true depends on how one sets out to determine it. Hence the debates which have arisen throughout history when scientific investigations have revealed *truths* which have contradicted the *truth* of the Bible.

Being honest or telling the truth means relating the facts as one knows and understands them. In the medical context this might mean that being honest is sometimes to admit to not knowing. For example, when the patient with inoperable carcinoma asks 'How long have I got?', the truthful answer is probably 'we do not know'. For the truth of the matter, the facts of the case are simply that the patient has a condition which is beyond the scope of medicine to cure and which will almost inevitably cause the patient's death. How long that process will take or whether the patient will die from some other cause in the meantime we do not know. It is important to distinguish between the truth – the facts of the case – and interpretation of, or opinion about, the facts. Professional opinion, be it medical, nursing, legal or theological, does not necessarily equate with truth.

Truth telling

We now turn to the question of whether one has a duty to tell the truth. In Chapter 1 we saw that in the course of normal social interaction it is accepted in society that in certain circumstances one need not tell the whole truth. Indeed it might be preferable not to do so if doing so would cause unnecessary distress. Nevertheless, it is a generally accepted notion that truth telling is a good thing. Kant, in his essay *On the Supposed Right to Tell Lies from Benevolent Motives*, concludes that 'to be truthful in all declarations is therefore a sacred unconditional command of reason, and not to be limited by any expediency'. Kant argues that to tell lies is wrong, because to do so always causes injury to another. It is important to note that he concludes that it is in *all declarations* that one should be truthful. In other words if you say anything it should be truthful or honest, but there is not necessarily a compunction to say anything.

How then are we to interpret these general ideas in the medical and nursing situation? Obviously the first point to emerge is that whatever we tell the patient should be the truth. There is no justification for telling a lie, a deliberate untruth. Do we, though, have the right to withhold information? Or do we have a duty to voluntarily tell the truth, i.e. even if the patient does not ask for it? There are two ways of approaching these questions. The first is from the standpoint of the doctor–patient, nurse–patient relationship and the effects that withholding information would have on that relationship. The second is from the standpoint of the patient's rights, in particular his right to information.

Veatch (1981) argues that if it became generally known that

doctors and nurses on occasion withheld information from their patients, then the effect this would have on their relationships with patients would be far-reaching. Patients would never know if they had been told the whole truth and would begin to mistrust any information they were given. Thus there would be a breakdown of trust in the patient–professional relationship, and trust is the very basis of that relationship.

If we accept the notion that the patient has a right to information about his diagnosis, treatment and prognosis, then the professional has a duty to give that information. It could further be argued that unless the patient clearly indicates that he does not wish to exert his right to information then the professional has a clear duty to provide him with it. The onus does not lie on the patient to ask but on the professional to tell.

Truth telling in terminal care

'It is an unpleasant task to tell a patient that his illness is terminal. One can understand why many doctors and nurses shirk this duty' (Varga 1980). If we accept Veatch's argument that to deceive the patient, either by telling an untruth or withholding the truth, is to undermine the professional-lay relationship, then it follows that there can be almost no exceptions to the rule. Even if the facts are that the disease is incurable and will inevitably lead to death, the duty of the professional is to tell the patient, the argument being that if it became generally known that patients were only told relatively good news then they would never know if they had been told the whole truth.

Nevertheless, in practice, patients are not always informed of their prognosis when it is very poor. The defence of not doing so is that such information would only increase anxiety and not benefit the patient. The Patients' Bill of Rights affirms that 'The patient has the right to obtain from his physician complete information concerning his diagnosis, treatment and prognosis in terms the patient can be reasonably expected to understand' (American Hospital Association 1972). That then would seem to clinch the argument. However, that same clause continues, 'When it is *not medically advisable* to give such information to the patient, the information should be made available to an appropriate person on his behalf' (my italics).

As we saw in Chapter 8 there are situations when, as in the case of a child or a severely mentally handicapped patient, to refrain from giving information to the patient and give it instead to a parent or near relative is justified. Unfortunately this clause in the Patients' Bill of Rights is often seen as a let out. Doctors can argue that it is not medically advisable to tell a patient he has a terminal illness because in their view the patient will not be able to take it or that to do so would be damaging to the patient. As a result the patient's family are informed and then the family, with the doctors and nurses, 'begin to play a game with the patient, concealing the truth and offering false hope' (Varga 1980). This then not only undermines the doctor–patient and nurse–patient relationship, but seriously damages the relationship between the patient and family. The family are forced into a situation of living a lie and may find it increasingly difficult to communicate with the patient at all. The case of Mr Williams illustrates this point.

Mr Williams, aged 72, was admitted to hospital suffering with chest pain and persistent cough. Exploratory surgery was undertaken and he was found to have inoperable carcinoma of the bronchus. The growth was left intact and the chest wall closed. Mr Williams was subsequently discharged home under the impression that when his general health improved he would be re-admitted for further surgery. His wife, however, was told the truth – that he had cancer and no curative treatment was possible. His condition was terminal. After a few weeks his condition slowly deteriorated and he began to remark that he did not seem to be getting any better, although he said the surgeon had told him he would.

Mrs Williams, afraid that he might ask questions which she would find difficult to answer, spent less and less time with him. She would only go into his room if he called, or to give him his meals and medication, and then would leave as quickly as possible. The couple had been married for over 50 years and had enjoyed a close, loving relationship which was now being destroyed.

One day, Mr Williams asked the district nurse point blank whether he was never going to get better. The nurse asked him what he thought, and then gently confirmed his suspicions that his condition was deteriorating and that there was nothing that could be done to prevent that process. The nurse then informed Mrs Williams of what had transpired and reassured her that her husband had accepted the information. From then on Mrs Williams spent most of her time sitting with Mr Williams and they enjoyed together the time he had left.

Had Mr Williams been told the truth in the first place then the couple would probably have been spared several weeks of loneliness and anguish.

According to ethical principles everybody has a right to the truth unless he decides that he does not want to be told it. The patient may indicate in some way that he does not want to be told the truth about his illness, in which case the doctor is under no moral obligation to tell him. Unless the patient does so indicate, the doctor's moral responsibility is clear; he should inform the patient. 'It seems to me that the physician should not easily assume that truthful information would be harmful to his patient. Non-communication could be actually more harmful than the truth' (Varga 1980). In the case of Mr Williams this was certainly so.

Generally the climate seems to be changing. Oken (1961) found that 91 per cent of physicians who responded to a questionnaire expressed a preference for not telling their patients that they had cancer. A survey carried out by the University of Rochester Medical Centre in 1979 (Varga 1980) found that 97 per cent of the doctors who responded expressed a preference for truthfully telling patients they had cancer.

Who decides?

Sometimes when a patient is found to have a terminal illness the doctor will decide not to tell the patient on the grounds that it is not 'medically advisable' or that as the patient has not asked he obviously does not want to know. If the decision is based on the former reason then it is inevitably very subjective. One can never be totally objectively certain what the effects of the information on the patient will be. To support the decision not to tell, doctors will quote cases of patients who having been told have 'given up', whose condition has deteriorated far more rapidly, and for whom death came sooner than expected. The question one has to ask is 'Does that matter?' Is it actually *harmful* to the patient? The patient, having been given the information, has the right to decide how to respond. It is the patient's right to decide to fight the disease, to live to their optimum level to the end, or to give up and let the disease and death take over. To say that this patient should not be told because 'he will not be able to take it' or 'he will lose the will to live' is to be guilty of paternalism.

If the decision not to tell is taken on the grounds that because the patient has not asked he does not want to know, then maybe to do so is on the basis of a false assumption. The reason the patient does not ask may not necessarily be that he does not want to know. It may be that the idea has not entered into his head. Consider, for example, a patient who is still young and relatively fit but has a condition which is going to be rapidly progressive, such as malignant melanoma which is not responding to treatment. If the decision to tell him is delayed until he is very ill, he may be angry that he was not told sooner when he was fit enough to be able to make arrangements for his family and business. He could rightly claim that he had been deceived, because although no-one had ever lied to him, nor had he ever asked the right questions, he had not been told the truth. The truth – the facts of the case – had been withheld from him until a time when he was unable to make good use of the information.

Sometimes it will be the patient's family who will decide the patient should not be told. Again, they will claim that they are doing so for the patient's benefit. They do not wish to cause him anxiety or distress or to take away hope. Unfortunately, it is false hope they are preserving, whereas if the patient has the information he can be given true hope: hope of a peaceful, dignified death, hope of living to the end, hope of the next life. While relatives may believe they are acting in the patient's best interests, the real reason for their not wanting to tell the patient may be their own difficulties in coming to terms with death, and fear of not being able to cope with the situation once it is out in the open. In view of their own emotional involvement it is doubtful if relatives are necessarily the best people to make this decision.

Although we as professionals may claim that it is the family who have decided that the patient should not be told, this is not strictly true. At some point the doctor has made the decision to tell the family before telling the patient. It may be that in so doing he is trying to shift the responsibility of deciding from himself to the family. It may be that he is fairly certain what their decision will be, and by electing to tell them has already elected not to tell the patient.

It should of course be the patient who decides whether he is to be told. After all the information is about him; it belongs to him. He more than anyone else has a right to it. The responsibility of the professional, doctor or nurse, is to try by careful questioning to elicit from the patient just how much, at any point in time, he wants to know.

Who should tell?

If it were general practice to tell the patients the whole truth about their condition, its treatment and prognosis, then perhaps this question would not need to be asked. The doctor is the person who arrives at the diagnosis and prognosis, and prescribes the treatment. Since he has the facts then it is his moral duty to pass them on to the patient. He might, justifiably, decide that in some instances the patient might cope better with the information if it were given to him by someone else, someone with whom the patient already had a close, trusting relationship.

The reason why the question 'Who should tell?' is so frequently raised is because so often the decision is made initially not to tell or to delay telling until the patient appears ready for it. As a result, several people in addition to the doctor know the facts; the relatives, the nurses, other members of the health care team all know. The patient is likely at some point to ask any one of them.

Bear in mind that we have already established certain moral principles. One, that truth telling is good and that to tell an untruth is wrong. Two, that to withhold truth is to deceive just as much as to tell a lie. Three, that nurses as much as doctors have a duty to tell patients the truth in order to maintain the professional–lay relationship and to uphold the fourth principle that patients have a right to information. Therefore, it would seem to follow that whomever the patient asks should answer truthfully, and if they have the relevant information they have a duty to impart it.

This author recently carried out a small survey of a group of experienced district nurses and a group of district nurse students.[1] The survey was designed to find out how nurses thought they should respond to a range of ethical dilemmas involving possible conflict between nurse and doctor. One of the situations with which respondents were presented was '*The doctor has explicitly stated that he does not want a terminally ill patient to be told his diagnosis and prognosis. During a routine nursing procedure the patient asks the nurse a direct question about his condition.*' Forty-six per cent of respondents thought the nurse should answer truthfully while 41.5 per cent thought the nurse should avoid answering the question. The remainder ticked the response 'don't know' or 'neither of these'. Almost half of those surveyed thought they should answer truthfully. It would of course be quite wrong to draw any firm conclusions or to generalize on the basis of such a limited survey. What concerns us here is the rightness or wrongness of the two suggested responses in this situation.

Let us consider first the suggestion that the nurse should avoid answering the question. If she were to say 'I don't know' when in fact she did know then she would be telling an untruth and this could subsequently undermine her relationship with the patient. If she tells the patient she cannot answer him and that he should ask the doctor, she has effectively answered him. He will almost certainly deduce that there must be something very wrong with him. The lack of a definite answer may well do him more harm than would certain knowledge of the truth.

If on the other hand the nurse answers the patient's questions truthfully and spends time with him, counselling him and helping him to come to terms with the information, then this may be far more beneficial to him. It is very doubtful that a nurse can effectively nurse a terminally ill patient unless there is an openness and sharing of information. One of the main aims in nursing the terminally ill is to help them toward a peaceful and dignified death. The nurse can do little or nothing toward achieving this aim unless the patient is aware of his condition. Thus, it would seem the nurse is morally justified in answering the patient truthfully.

However, either response – to tell the truth or to go along with the doctor's decision not to tell – can be morally defended. The nurse in this situation does face a very real moral dilemma, between on the one hand responding to the patient's right to know, and on the other complying with the doctor's wish to spare the patient anxiety. The UKCC Code of Professional Conduct (1984) states the nurse shall 'work in a collaborative and co-operative manner with other health care professionals and recognise and respect their particular contributions within the health care team'. From which it would seem that the nurse has a moral responsibility to comply with the doctor's wishes.

In each given situation the nurse has to decide which course of action will benefit the patient most and cause least harm. Professional codes of ethics, however good, have their limitations. It is impossible to derive a code which will provide explicit answers to every individual situation. 'It is a mistake to think that all a conscientious nurse needs in order to deal with the moral dilemmas that arise in nursing is an adequate code of ethics coupled with a healthy measure of common sense' (Benjamin and Curtis 1981). At the end of the day the nurse carries personal responsibility for what she does and she, not the doctor, nor anyone else, must make the final decision.

Ideally, situations like that which we have been discussing can be avoided. If there were full and open discussion between the members of the caring team then there would be no way in which one member of the team would be able to take a unilateral decision which might subsequently pose a moral dilemma for other members of the team. It is becoming common practice on terminal care units for the whole caring team, including sometimes the chaplain, to debate and agree jointly whether, when, and how the patient should be told. Would this were common practice in all situations!

Further points for discussion

Our concern in this chapter has been with truth telling and, in the specific area of terminal care, with who should tell the truth to the patient. Since truth telling is a basic moral principle, then it seems almost obligatory that doctors, nurses and other health workers should always tell patients the truth about their condition. Coupled with this we have the now fairly firmly established principle that patients have a right to information. On the face of it then the answer to the question should patients be told is a firm *yes*. However, the dilemma that we face is balancing these two principles against others such as the duty to prevent harm, pain or anxiety to patients in our care. It may well be that in some situations the truth may actually cause the patient to suffer more pain and anxiety than not knowing it.

It can be argued that in some circumstances the right course of action would be to withhold the truth, e.g. when a patient who has had a malignant tumour which has been removed surgically is now making a good recovery. To tell the patient that he had had cancer might well be detrimental to his recovery and in the long term cause him considerable anxiety. In the minds of many lay people cancer is still synonymous with death, and they may not believe that in their case this is not so. True, one can never give a carte blanche assurance that it will never return, that there will be no secondary growths, but nevertheless, in many instances it would be true to say that life expectancy following successful treatment of a primary growth was good. Why then, the argument goes, cause the patient a life-time of unnecessary anxiety and doubt when his health prospects are very good? It is obviously dangerous to try and arrive at a rule to be applied in every situation.

I have in this chapter concentrated on telling the truth in terminal illness. Of course telling people that they have cancer or are terminally ill are not the only occasions when the truth is hard to tell and hard to hear. Consider the effects on a person of being told that they have multiple sclerosis, rheumatoid arthritis or some other chronic, debilitating disease. Should they be told their diagnosis when still in the early stages of the disease, when their symptoms are relatively minor and causing them little discomfort or inconvenience? I leave it to the reader to explore the possible responses to that question.

Some would argue that the question whether to tell or not to tell becomes redundant when viewed in the context of the Nursing Process. Inherent in the Nursing Process is the idea that patients should be involved in their own assessment of needs and planning of care. The nurse, if she assesses accurately the patient's needs, should be able to tell when the patient is ready to receive information. In reality, however, the situation is more complex. The nurse may still be under pressure from either the doctor or the patient's relatives not to impart some specific information. The Nursing Process philosophy merely provides the nurse with moral justification for going against the wishes of doctor or relatives; it does not alter the fact that she still faces a moral dilemma.

We have seen that the nurse, as much as the doctor, has a duty to tell the truth, to uphold the patient's right to information and therefore must herself decide whether to tell or not to tell. Each individual carries personal responsibility for their own moral decisions, and to use as a defence 'someone else told me to' is morally no defence at all. In the next chapter we shall explore further the nurse–doctor relationship and some of the moral dilemmas faced by nurses which might cause conflict within that relationship.

Notes

1 The findings of this survey and their implications are further discussed in Chapter 11.

References

American Hospital Association (1972), *A Patients' Bill of Rights.*
Benjamin, M. and Curtis, J. (1981), *Ethics in Nursing*, New York: Oxford University Press.
Kant, I. translated by Abbott, T.K. (1909), 'On the Supposed Right to Tell Lies from Benevolent Motives', cited in Veatch, R.M. (1981), *A Theory of Medical Ethics*, New York: Basic Books.
Oken, D. (1961), cited in Varga, A.C. (1980), *The Main Issues in Bioethics*, New York: Paulist Press.
Oppenheimer, J.R. (1955), cited in Salzman, L. (1973), 'Truth, Honesty and the Therapeutic Process'. In Gorovitz, S. et al (eds) (1976) *Moral Problems in Medicine*, Englewood Cliffs, N.J.: Prentice-Hall.
Salzman, L. (1973), 'Truth Honesty and the Therapeutic Process'. In Gorovitz, S. et al (eds), (1976), *Moral Problems in Medicine*, New York: Prentice-Hall.
Varga, A.C. (1980), *The Main Issues in Bioethics*, New York: Paulist Press.
Veatch, R.M. (1981), *A Theory of Medical Ethics*, New York: Basic Books.
UKCC (United Kingdom Central Council for Nursing, Midwifery and Health Visiting) (1984), *Code of Professional Conduct for the Nurse, Midwife and Health Visitor*, 2nd Edition, London: UKCC.

Further reading

Gorovitz, S. et al (eds) (1976), *Moral Problems in Medicine*, New Jersey: Prentice-Hall Inc. See in particular papers on 'Truth-Telling', pp. 94ff.
Reich, W.T. (ed) (1978), *Encyclopedia of Bioethics*, New York: Macmillan and Free Press. See especially the following articles: 'Truth-telling: Attitudes', Veatch, R.M.; 'Truth-Telling: Ethical Aspects', Bok, S.
Stedeford, A. (1984), *Facing Death*, London: William Heinemann Medical Books. See Chapters 3, 4 and 5.
Summers, R. (1984), Should Patients be Told More?, *Nursing Mirror*, August 29, Vol. 159, No. 7, pp. 16–20.
Thompson, I. (ed) (1979), *Dilemmas of Dying*, a study in the ethics of terminal care, Edinburgh: Edinburgh University Press.
Veatch, R.M. (1977), *Case Studies in Medical Ethics*, Cambridge, Mass.: Harvard University Press.

11

THE NURSE–DOCTOR RELATIONSHIP

> In my estimation obedience is the first law and the very cornerstone of good nursing. And here is the first stumbling block for the beginner. No matter how gifted she may be, she will never become a reliable nurse until she can obey without question. The first and most helpful criticism I ever received from a doctor was when he told me that I was supposed to be simply an intelligent machine for the purpose of carrying out his orders.
> *Dock 1917*

According to Dock, then, a good nurse was one who obeyed the doctor's instructions without question. She did not see the nurse as having even the slightest hint of ethical autonomy. It seems strange to us now that even 70 years ago anyone could suggest that a group of individuals by virtue of their role should be expected to totally abdicate their moral rights and responsibilities. Even the Jesuits, bound by their strict vows of obedience, have never been expected to obey their superior if he ordered them to commit a sin.

Surely then it is totally unreasonable for a doctor to expect a nurse to obey his instructions if these require her to do a morally wrong act. The question of truth telling, discussed in the previous chapter, is a case in point. A doctor cannot expect a nurse to lie to a patient simply because he has told her to do so. Nevertheless, nearly half the nurses in my sample referred to in Chapter 10 said that they would comply with a doctor's instructions not to tell the truth (Table 1), although not actually telling an untruth.

The underlying question to many of the conflicts which arise within the nurse–doctor relationship is 'Should a nurse always obey a doctor?' For Dock, and others like her, 60 to a 100 years ago, the answer was definitely 'yes'. Even as late as 1965 we find a revised edition of Morison's *Stepping Stones to Professional Growth* stating that the nurse must follow orders and uphold the physician's professional reputation.

It is not altogether surprising that *obedience* should have become to be seen as an essential attribute of nurses. Historically, at least in

Table 1 Telling the truth.

Possible response	Number	Per cent
The nurse should answer truthfully	19	46
The nurse should avoid answering the question	17	42
Don't know/neither of these	5	12

Europe, the two major influences on nursing have been the religious orders of the Middle Ages and the Army of the 19th century. In both, the idea of unquestioning obedience is paramount. Furthermore, traditionally, nurses have been female and doctors male. This led in the past to the one profession becoming subservient to the other. However, the influence of the feminist movement has done much to redress the balance.

Generally, the climate has changed. Nurses are no longer taught to carry out unquestioningly doctors' instructions. It is now recognized that nurses have professional responsibility for their own actions. 'The nurse assumes responsibility and accountability for individual nursing judgements and actions' (American Nurses' Association 1976). This transition from a reacting profession carrying out its activities in response to doctors' orders to an independent one has increased rather than decreased the range of ethical dilemmas faced by nurses. All the time that nurses were expected to obey without question the orders of doctors life was relatively simple. Nurses could disclaim responsibility for the results of their actions if they were only doing as they were told. True they might have experienced some internal personal conflict but they could justify their actions by saying 'I don't personally think it is right but I am doing what I am told and as I have no right to question I cannot be held responsible.' Once nurses began to assume or be given responsibility for their own actions then they had to decide themselves whether an action was right or wrong and act accordingly.

The *professionalization* of nursing has meant that nurses are no longer taught that they are, nor do they see themselves as, doctors' handmaids. Nurses have become independent decision makers, making decisions about the most appropriate nursing intervention in each case. It is not only with respect to nursing care that nurses must take responsibility for their decisions and actions but also with respect to medical directives. In law it is no defence to say that you acted on the instructions of another and disclaim responsibility for your actions. Morally it is certainly no defence. Morally both he who gives instructions and he who carries them out are equally responsible.

Nevertheless 'Should nurses always obey doctors?' is still the question at the centre of many conflicts in the nurse–doctor relationship.

Clinical judgement

One area in which conflict might arise is where the nurse doubts or disagrees with a clinical decision made by a doctor, e.g. if she feels that the prescribed treatment might be harmful to the patient. The nurse then has to decide between her obligation to the doctor (to ensure that the prescribed medical treatment is carried out) and her obligation to the patient (to protect him from harm). 'Whatever the strength of the historical legacy and the dominating status of medicine, whenever a nurse faces a choice between obligation to a physician and obligation to a client she must recognise that her obligation to a client is primary' (Benjamin and Curtis 1981).

Suppose a doctor has given a patient a prescription for a drug which the district nurse is to administer. When the nurse arrives at the house she reads the doctor's instructions and is certain that the dosage exceeds the recommended level. Clearly in this situation the nurse has a duty to check whether the prescribed dosage is within safe limits before she administers it. To give it when she has even the slightest doubt would be wrong. If it were an excessive dosage and some harm subsequently befell the patient then she would be as guilty as the doctor of causing harm to the patient. In the survey already referred to, all the respondents said they would not give the drug without first checking the dosage with either the doctor or pharmacist (Table 2).

Let us then take this a stage further. Suppose the nurse queries the dosage with the doctor who, without referring to the literature, gives the nurse an assurance that there is no need to worry. If she still has doubts then she should check the information herself and if she then discovers the dosage to be incorrect, inform the doctor and refuse to administer the drug. If, on the other hand, she takes the doctor's word for it and, trusting in his judgement, administers the drug then she could still be held to share liability if it has an adverse effect on

Table 2 Questioning treatment prescribed by a doctor.

	Number	*Per cent*
The nurse suspects that the prescribed dosage of a drug exceeds the recommended level		
The nurse should:		
give the drug and say nothing	0	0
give the drug and then query it	0	0
not give the drug until cleared with the pharmacist	1	2
not give the drug until cleared with the doctor	40	98
don't know/none of these	0	0
Treatment ordered as 'experiment'		
The nurse should:		
carry out the treatment	12	29
refuse to carry out the treatment	15	37
don't know/neither of these	14	34
Giving a placebo		
The nurse should:		
carry out the treatment	28	68
refuse to carry out the treatment	4	10
don't know/neither of these	9	22

Total responses, both groups ($n = 41$).

the patient. It could be argued that as a professional person she should not rely on another's assumed knowledge but should have that knowledge herself.

In this type of situation perhaps the best course of action would be for the nurse initially to check the facts before questioning the doctor. By so doing she would be fulfilling her obligation to the patient and, at the same time, reducing the possibility of conflict with the doctor by at least questioning his judgement from a firm basis.

Probably few would argue with the notion that the nurse should question the doctor's clinical judgement when it involves the possibility of harm to the patient. In not all situations are the consequences so obviously harmful as in the case of a drug overdose.

Another situation posed in the questionnaire was: '*The doctor has prescribed a treatment for a patient which the nurse feels is unnecessary, i.e. it will not improve the patient's condition. She suspects it has been ordered as either (a) an experiment, or (b) a placebo.*'

Respondents were divided in their answers to (*a*) with 29 per cent ticking the response 'The nurse should carry out the treatment' and 37 per cent the response 'The nurse should refuse to carry out the treatment'. In response to (*b*) the majority, 68 per cent, thought the nurse should carry out the treatment and 10 per cent that she should refuse.

The ethics of experimentation on patients were discussed in Chapter 8; there it was established that to carry out experiments on patients which would not benefit them was unethical and that to do so without their informed consent was wrong. If in this situation the nurse's suspicion is correct (i.e. that the treatment ordered is an experiment and that it will not benefit the patient), then she would be acting in the best interests of the patient by refusing to carry out the treatment. Clearly the nurse should attempt to ascertain if her suspicion is correct before making a decision whether or not to carry out the treatment. While she has doubts then she would be justified in refusing to carry out the treatment.

The question of giving placebos is a complex one. On the one hand it is argued that giving a placebo benefits the patient inasmuch as it puts his mind at rest and he 'feels better'; on the other hand it is argued that it is a quite deliberate act of deception. There is little doubt that those who prescribe and administer placebos do so thinking that the patient is being deceived. It may well be that the patient sees through the deception but, nevertheless, the intention to deceive is there. What the nurse has to decide is whether the benefit to the patient is such that it outweighs the act of deception.

In this, as in the majority of moral dilemmas, there is seldom a clear-cut *right* answer. One person may weigh the two sides of the argument and come to the opposite answer to another. The doctor may consider that the benefit to the patient is sufficient to warrant the act of deception. The nurse may not. Moral decisions have to be made by each individual.

Within the context of the nurse–doctor relationship the issues are further compounded by the way in which that relationship is perceived. 'A physician who sees himself as an independent omnipotent man with mystical healing powers relates to co-workers as he does to patients and therefore insists that nurses and other health providers serve him in his so-called "captain of the ship" role' (Kalisch and Kalisch 1977). The doctor may take the stance 'Okay, you may not agree with me, but what I say goes'.

The nurse, in essence, faces a double problem. She has first to decide whether or not a particular action, such as giving a placebo, is right. She then has to decide whether she should obey the doctor. Nurses have traditionally obeyed doctors and doctors expect nurses to carry out their orders. In refusing to obey the nurse is going against the traditional norms of behaviour and also the doctor's expectations of her.

Obviously there are circumstances in which obedience is necessary. In an emergency situation, such as a cardiac arrest, it is essential that someone assumes control and others respond to his or her orders. Nurses, doctors and other health workers have to be able to react quickly and responsively to orders. This forms an essential part of their training. People who are trained to respond quickly to orders in some situations may find it difficult to do other than obey in other situations.

The doctor is responsible for the medical care and treatment of the patient. He is obviously more knowledgeable about medical care than is the nurse. Therefore, it can be argued that nurses should follow doctors' orders because it is reasonable to expect them to be correct, and that the patient is more likely to benefit if she does so than if she does not. However, doctors are human and fallible and their judgements can be wrong. If the nurse unquestioningly carries out all medical orders it could result in harm to the patient. 'In so far as a nurse has an obligation to follow a doctor's orders it is only a prima facie obligation and may be overridden in certain circumstances by other factors. A nurse must be careful not to confuse a well-grounded prima facie obligation with blind faith' (Benjamin and Curtis 1981).

Specialist and extended roles

There have been two important developments in nursing in recent years: the emergence of the *specialist nurse* and the *extended role* of the nurse. These expansions of the traditional role of the nurse have increased the likelihood of conflict within the nurse–doctor relationship, and have done so chiefly in two ways.

Firstly, nurses having acquired this expansion of their knowledge and skills feel more able to question the decisions of doctors. The specialist nurse may, quite justifiably, feel that her knowledge in her field is superior to that of a particular doctor. The nurse is working within the speciality, say terminal care, on a daily basis and dealing almost exclusively with the terminally ill. The doctor, on the other hand, may be new to this work or may only be treating a handful of terminally ill patients amongst a varied case load. Furthermore, the nurse generally spends more time with each patient than does the doctor and so is in a better position to know his individual needs, preferences, hopes and anxieties. The nurse may indeed be better able than the doctor to judge what is the most appropriate care for the patient.

What then if the nurse is firmly of the opinion that the doctor's suggested treatment is not the most appropriate? The first question the nurse needs to ask herself is 'to what extent is the treatment the doctor has ordered *nursing* care and to what extent is it *medical* care?' Clearly, the nurse is better able than the doctor to assess nursing needs and prescribe nursing care. She would be failing in her duty to the patient if she carried out nursing care which she considered either inappropriate or inadequate. Equally clearly, the doctor, rather than the nurse, is better able to assess medical needs and prescribe medical care. The nurse may not agree with his decisions; she might say, 'that is not what I would do', in which case she would be justified in discussing her thoughts with the doctor. However, unless the treatment is harmful to the patient she should, at the end of the day, comply with the doctor's instructions. The nurse, however specialized, is a specialist in nursing in her particular field. She is not a medical specialist. It is extremely important that nurses, as indeed all professionals, should recognize their limitations.

The second area of conflict might arise from role expectation. Doctors, aware that there is something called *the extended role of the nurse* and that nurses can now perform certain tasks formerly considered to be medical, might expect that all nurses can perform those tasks. Doctors may not be aware of (or if they are might think them petty) the regulations governing the extended role of the nurse. In the United Kingdom quite clear regulations exist which make requirements of the nurse, the employing authority and the doctor. The nurse's role can be legally extended in the following circumstances:

1 The nurse has been specifically and adequately trained for the performance of the new task and she agrees to undertake it.
2 This training has been recognised as satisfactory by the employing authority.
3 The new task has been recognised by the profession and by the employing authority as a task which may be properly delegated to a nurse.
4 The delegating doctor has been assured of the competence of the individual nurse concerned.
DHSS 1977

If all concerned are fully aware of and comply with the regulations there should, in theory, be no conflict. Nevertheless, conflicts do arise. Consider the following situation.

Sister Johnson whilst working for Health Authority A receives training in, and is given a certificate of competence to perform, venepuncture. She continues in their employment for a few years during which time she frequently carries out this procedure. After three years she moves and takes up employment with Health Authority B. She is not allowed by her new employers to carry out this procedure until she undertakes their training and they are assured of her competence to do the task. This Sister Johnson accepts although she thinks it a little absurd. After all, her new employers are more than happy for her to carry out procedures she learned during her basic training and yet has not practised for some time.

Doctor Phillips, the general practitioner with whom Sister Johnson now works, asks her one day to take a sample of blood from a patient whom she is about to visit. Sister Johnson explains the situation to him. Dr Phillips says 'Just this once won't matter. I am confident in your ability to do it and you've had plenty of experience. Don't worry, if there is any come-back I will back you up.'

When the nurses in the survey were posed this type of situation 95 per cent ticked the response 'The nurse should refuse to carry out the procedure' (Table 3). It might be easy to assume from this result that the situation posed no real dilemma, that the decision to refuse was clear-cut. Let us consider the possible consequences, firstly, of refusing to carry out the procedure and, secondly, of agreeing to do so.

Sister Johnson is new to the area; she has recently joined the health care team and is keen to build good working relationships within the team. She also has ideas that she hopes to implement and for which she will need the cooperation of the general practitioners,

Table 3   Conflict arising from extended role.

	Number	*Per cent*
Doctor asks nurse to carry out procedure for which she is not 'certificated' by her employing authority		
The nurse should:		
refuse to carry out the procedure	39	95
agree to carry out procedure	2	5
don't know	0	0

including Dr Phillips. In refusing to do 'a favour' for Dr Phillips she may have jeopardized future working relationships. Her refusal might be interpreted as non-cooperation. Her refusal might consequently be detrimental to patient care. So one might conclude that she could be justified in carrying out the procedure, at least on this one occasion. However, the argument is somewhat conjectural.

What then if she were to carry out the procedure? Obviously if it were discovered by her employer that she had done so she would be liable to disciplinary action. She has obligations to her employer which are both moral and legal. While in some circumstances it is possible to argue a very strong moral case for breaking the law, in this particular situation it most definitely is not. Suppose, too, that as a result of Sister Johnson taking this patient's blood the patient is harmed in some way. Suppose he becomes infected, or because Sister Johnson incorrectly handles the specimen the results of the test are invalidated, then whatever Dr Phillips has said about backing her up, she would be personally accountable for the outcome of her actions.

The extended role of the nurse is of course about much more than performing particular *tasks*. Although on the surface the conflict may appear to be about the task, it is underlaid by a difference in interpretation of *role*. Role can be defined in terms of the rights and obligations accorded to the incumbent of a particular position.

While the DHSS regulations of 1977 at the time of writing still stand, thinking within the professions has moved on. More emphasis now tends to be placed on the individual nurse's right to decide whether she is *competent* to do something rather than the possession of a certificate. Furthermore the document itself did acknowledge the rights of the individual professionals involved. The doctor has the right to refuse to delegate, regardless of the agreement of the Health Authority or the nurse's ability to carry out the procedure. Equally, the nurse has the right to decline to accept the delegation. She may do so on the grounds that she does not feel competent or has not been taught how to carry out the procedure. She may also do so on a specific occasion if she considers that in giving time to carrying out the delegated task she would be putting at risk nursing care to other patients (she may, for example, be alone on the ward at the time).

Many of the conflicts between the nurse and doctor still arise from the doctor's expectation that the nurse is there to do his bidding. One district nurse told me that the general practitioners with whom she worked expected her to do all electrocardiograms. They expected the nurse to visit a patient for the sole purpose of performing an ECG. There was no *nursing* reason for her to visit. The conflict here is not about whether or not nurses should perform the task, nor over a difference of opinion as to whether the procedure is necessary, but about the *role* of the nurse. It is about whether the nurse's role is to carry out doctors' orders or to provide expert nursing knowledge and skills.

The autonomy of the nurse

The role of the nurse has developed in a far more fundamental way than the taking on of previously medical tasks. Over the past two decades the nursing profession has begun to develop a knowledge base which is its own. The re-examination of *what is nursing* has led to the development of a philosophy which in turn has provided that approach to nursing care known as the Nursing Process. For the first time in its history nursing now has the beginnings of a unique body of knowledge and can therefore define the scope of nursing skills.

Nursing actions are no longer determined solely on the basis of the medical diagnosis but also the nursing diagnosis. Clearly in planning and giving nursing care the nurse cannot ignore the medical condition of the patient, but that is only one factor among many which the nurse has to take into account. 'We as nurses make a contribution to the care of the patient which can be quite independent of the doctor. This independent function is well illustrated in the care of the terminally ill patient, who by definition cannot be "cured" by medical treatment' (Hargreaves 1979).

The implementation of the Nursing Process can, and sadly does, lead to conflict between nurse and doctor. For example, the doctor may consider that there is no medical reason for a patient remaining in hospital and order his discharge. The nurse may consider that the patient still requires nursing care, and that, until adequate resources can be organized in the patient's home, he should continue to be nursed in hospital. The doctor, however, may want the bed for another patient.

Another example is where a doctor 'prescribes' nursing care which the nurse considers inappropriate. It is still all too frequent for a general practitioner to visit a patient at home, and inform the patient that he will send the nurse in to bathe him, or carry out some other specific nursing task. When the district nurse subsequently visits the patient and assesses his needs she may conclude that the care 'ordered' by the doctor is inappropriate. This can, in the first instance, lead to a difficult situation for the nurse to handle with the patient; it can also lead to conflict between doctor and nurse.

Because of the historical background it can be difficult for nurses to establish their autonomy. Conflict, such as in the examples cited, can arise for one of two main reasons. It can, on the one hand, be because the individual doctor refuses to accept the notion of nursing autonomy, and sees the Nursing Process as a lot of unnecessary paper work which prevents *his* nurse from giving *his* patients the care he thinks they need. On the other hand, and all too frequently, it is because the nurse has either failed to fully explain what is the Process, or implements it badly or discourteously.

My own observations, in both the hospital and community settings, are that some nurses still only pay lip service to the Nursing Process. The documentation is completed, but there is little relationship between the information in the nursing history and care plan and what is actually implemented. Unless nurses show themselves to be committed to the Process and implement it fully, doctors are not likely to recognize its worth.

Where the Nursing Process is being well implemented, doctors recognize its value and respect the opinions and decisions of nurses. One ward Sister told me that the doctors on her ward routinely consulted the nursing records and discussed with the nursing staff the nursing needs of the patients before making decisions about the overall care of the patient. Decisions, such as when to discharge a patient, were made jointly.

Conflicts in interpersonal relationships, in most cases, arise from *how* things are said and done. In many cases, conflict related to role perception can be avoided by good communication. If nursing is to progress along the road to professional autonomy, it is reliant on nurses themselves being able to put their case across in an acceptable manner.

Divided loyalties

The sort of situations we have been discussing highlight another source of conflict in the nurse–doctor relationship. Nurses are employees of a Health Authority and through the nursing hierarchy have obligations to their employer. Doctors are employed on a different basis and they do not work within the sort of hierarchical structure that nurses do. The medical profession operates a 'collegial approach which accepts each doctor as a professional who gives and seeks advice among colleagues, and is open to judgment by his peers, but who is not held accountable for his day-to-day work to a management hierarchy' (Thompson et al 1983). The doctor, therefore, has a greater degree of independence than does the nurse. Doctors sometimes find it difficult to understand the pressures nurses experience as a consequence of their employee–employer relationship. Frequently, too, doctors resent what they see as interference by the nursing hierarchy in the care of *their* patients. This can make life more difficult for the individual nurse who feels under a duty to comply with requests and instructions from nurse management and, at the same time, a loyalty toward the doctor alongside whom she works. Nurses may actually find themselves being pulled in several directions; for apart from owing loyalty to the doctor and their nursing hierarchy, they also owe loyalty to the patients and their nursing colleagues.

Whenever conflict arises, the nurse must look first at her duty toward the patient whose needs are paramount. However, that is easier said than done, for the patient is the one who has the least power. The employing authority, represented by the nursing hierarchy, probably has the most power, for they have the power to instigate formal disciplinary procedures and ultimately to fire the nurse. The doctors' powers lie in the fact that good relationships between nurses and doctors are essential to a high standard of patient care, and to maximizing job satisfaction for the nurse. A breakdown in that relationship can make life unpleasant. Thus nurses work in an unenviable situation which compounds rather than eases their moral decision making.

Professional loyalty

From time to time patients will voice criticisms of the doctor to the nurse. (They may also criticize other nurses or other health workers and although the discussion here deals specifically with criticisms or complaints about doctors, the principles apply equally to those about other professionals.) If the nurse considers the criticism or complaint to be unjustified then clearly she experiences no conflict. She can honestly answer the criticism and rise to the defence of the doctor. It is when she feels that the criticism is or might be justified that the dilemma arises. Consider the following case.

During the course of a visit to a patient to give nursing care, the patient complains to the district nurse about the general practitioner. The patient says that the doctor was rude and appeared indifferent towards her. 'He rushed in here and told me off for calling him out. He didn't seem at all interested in anything I had to say.'

As with so many problem situations the nurse has first to decide what to do on the spot and subsequently how to follow up the problem.

One possible immediate response would be for the nurse to defend the doctor, saying, for example, that he was probably very busy and did not intentionally give the impression of disinterest. Alternatively, she could agree with the patient saying 'I know he's like that but he is very good clinically', or she could go a stage further and suggest the patient lodge an official complaint.

In the reality of the situation the nurse's response would probably be largely determined by her knowledge of the particular patient and doctor, and whether this was one of a series of similar complaints or a 'one-off' occurrence. The indications from my survey would tend to suggest that the immediate response of most would be to rise to the defence of the doctor. Ninety-three per cent of respondents ticked the response 'The nurse should defend the doctor', while none thought the nurse should agree with the patient, and the remaining 7 per cent ticked the response 'Don't know/neither of these'. The immediate response to rise to the defence of a professional is probably instinctive and not based on an analysis of the ethics of the situation.

Let us then try to establish a theoretical basis for making decisions about this type of dilemma. Nursing codes place emphasis on protecting the patient from harm and acting in the patient's best interests. For example: 'Act always in such a way as to promote and safeguard the well-being and interests of patients/clients' (UKCC 1984); 'The nurse acts to safeguard the client and the public when health care and safety are affected by the incompetence, unethical or illegal practice of any person' (American Nurses' Association 1976); and 'the nurse takes appropriate action to safeguard the individual when his care is endangered by a co-worker or any other person' (International Council of Nurses 1973). Furthermore, 'The patient has the right to considerate and respectful care' (American Hospital Association 1972).

From such statements one could argue that the nurse's duty in cases such as that under discussion would be to support the patient. Certainly if the nurse considered that the doctor's behaviour had been *incompetent* or *unethical* and such as to *endanger the care* of the patient, then she has a duty to act on behalf of the patient. If in this case the patient's account of the doctor's behaviour is true, then he has infringed the patient's right to *respectful care*. The appropriate response of the nurse would therefore be to advise the patient of how to proceed with an official complaint.

On the other hand, one could argue, though rather tenuously, from the same nursing codes that the nurse should defend the doctor and try to dissuade the patient from taking the complaint further. The nurse should 'work in a collaborative and cooperative manner with other health care professionals and recognise and respect their particular contributions within the health care team' (UKCC 1984) and 'the nurse sustains a cooperative relationship with co-workers in nursing and other fields' (International Council of Nurses 1973). Obviously the nurse should not take at face value patients' criticisms about professional colleagues. She should first try to ascertain the extent to which criticisms and complaints can be substantiated before voicing an opinion but she should remember that her duties and responsibilities to the patient are at all times paramount, and those to colleagues secondary.

The nurse, having decided on how to respond to the patient, then has to decide whether and how to follow up the incident. However the nurse decides to respond to the patient she cannot leave it there. She must follow it up by bringing the complaint to the doctor, or other professional, concerned. This view was supported by the majority in my survey; 75 per cent of those who answered the question said the nurse should subsequently confront the doctor with the complaint, while 17 per cent said they did not know. Whether or not the nurse considers the complaint to be justified she owes it to the doctor concerned to tell him what the patient has said about him.

If the complaint is unjustified and the nurse does not bring it to the doctor's attention the patient may voice his complaint to all and sundry which could be detrimental to the doctor's reputation. At least if he knows about it he can see the patient and try to resolve the situation. If the complaint is justified then equally the nurse has a duty to inform the doctor of what has transpired, because she has a duty to promote high standards of patient care and this must include confronting co-workers when she believes their standards to be less than adequate.

Situations such as that under discussion clearly need to be handled with tact and courtesy. For the nurse to 'take sides' may be unproductive and jeopardize her relationship with either the patient or doctor. It might be appropriate in the first instance for the nurse to explore the situation with the patient, neither defending the doctor nor siding with the patient. She might then tactfully approach the doctor, who might recognize that he had been rather abrupt on this occasion and apologize to the patient. However, patients have a right to expect nurses and doctors to be courteous and treat them with respect, and therefore nurses and doctors have a duty to behave in that way. However tired a doctor or nurse may be, however difficult and fraught their previous consultation may have been, or however busy they are, nothing can exempt them from the duty to treat each individual patient with the consideration he or she deserves.

Summary

Conflict within the nurse–doctor relationship arises largely because of the way in which that relationship is perceived. The historical legacy of the nurse being subservient to the doctor still influences the way in which many doctors and some nurses perceive the relationship. The results of my survey, though in no way conclusive, would tend to suggest that nurses are prepared to challenge doctors on some issues.

The changing role of the nurse and developments in nurse education have given nurses a greater sense of professional autonomy and greater confidence in their own knowledge base. As a consequence, the chances of conflicts arising between nurses and doctors have increased and nurses find themselves more often in the position of deciding between acting in obedience to the doctor and acting independently.

Good nursing care is to a large extent dependent on good relationships within the health care team. In few instances can any one member of the team function without the cooperation of others in the team. The nurse may find herself faced with the dilemma of either risking conflict for the benefit of one patient, which might be detrimental to working relationships and so adversely affect the care of other patients, or avoiding conflict to the detriment of one patient, but promoting cooperation and possibly enhancing patient care in the long term. In considering a response to this dilemma I refer the reader to earlier discussions, particularly those on *ends* and *means* in Chapter 1 and acting *for the good of the individual or many* in Chapter 4.

Whatever choice a nurse makes, be it in accord with a doctor's orders or in contradiction to them, she remains individually accountable for her actions. The nurse cannot say 'I acted that way because the doctor said so' and leave it at that. She has to be able to justify why she chose to obey the doctor, just as much as if she chose not to obey him. The nurse is professionally and morally accountable for her own actions.

References

American Hospital Association (1972), *A Patients' Bill of Rights.*
American Nurses' Association (1976), *Code for Nurses.*
Benjamin, M. and Curtis, J. (1981), *Ethics in Nursing*, New York: Oxford University Press.
DHSS (1977), 'The Extending Role of the Clinical Nurse – Legal Implications and Training Requirements', HC (77) 22, cited in Young, A.P. (1981), *Legal Problems in Nursing Practice*, London: Harper & Row.
Dock, S. (1917), The Relation of the Nurse to the Doctor and the Doctor to the Nurse, *American Journal of Nursing*, Vol. 17, p. 394, cited in Benjamin, M. and Curtis, J. (1981), *Ethics in Nursing*, New York: Oxford University Press.
Hargreaves, I. (1979), 'Theoretical Considerations'. In Kratz, C. (ed), *The Nursing Process*, London: Baillière Tindall.
International Council of Nurses (1973), *Code for Nurses*, Geneva: ICN.

Kalisch, B. and Kalisch, P. (1977), 'An Analysis of the Sources of Physician–Nurse Conflict', cited in Benjamin, M. and Curtis, J. (1981), *Ethics in Nursing*, New York: Oxford University Press.

Thompson, I.E., Melia, K.M. and Boyd, K.M. (1983), *Nursing Ethics*, Edinburgh: Churchill Livingstone.

UKCC (United Kingdom Central Council for Nursing, Midwifery and Health Visiting) (1984), *Code of Professional Conduct for the Nurse, Midwife, and Health Visitor*, 2nd Edition, London: UKCC.

Further reading

Chaska, N.L. (ed) (1978), *The Nursing Profession: Views Through the Mist*, New York: McGraw-Hill. See especially 'Nurse–Physician Relationships: Problems and Solutions', Hoekelman, R.A., pp. 330–335.

Beardshaw, V. (1981), *Conscientious Objectors at Work*, London: Social Audit.

Benjamin, M. and Curtis, J. (1981), *Ethics in Nursing*, New York: Oxford University Press. See in particular Chapter 4 on 'Recurring Ethical Issues in Nurse–Physician Relationships'.

Lawrence, J. and Crisham, P. (1984), 'Making a Choice' and 'A Study in Resolutions', *Nursing Times*, July 18, pp. 57–58, and July 25, pp. 53–55.

12

THE RIGHTS OF THE NURSE

For the most part the emphasis so far has been on the rights of the patient and the duties of the nurse toward the patient. When there has been discussion of the rights and responsibilities of the nurse it has been within the context of interpersonal relationships, nurse–patient or nurse–doctor relationships. In this chapter we shall be concerned chiefly with the rights, and to some extent the duties and responsibilities, of the nurse in a wider context. Two further topics are discussed, namely, the relationship between morality and the law, and the value and limitations of professional codes of ethics. The chapter concludes with some thoughts on ethical decision making.

In Chapter 5 we saw that there are different types of rights – *option rights* and *welfare rights*. We also saw that rights are not unlimited. Restrictions may be imposed, either because the exercise of one's right to do something might impinge upon another right of someone else, or because one also has a duty to behave in a particular way. A nurse, as a human being, shares with all other human beings certain option rights, and as a citizen of a particular society she shares with her fellow citizens certain welfare rights.

Now, given that rights are not unlimited, the question is 'Does being a nurse in itself impose limits on any of a person's rights?' The answer is that to some extent it must do. For one reason, in becoming a nurse, a person accepts certain duties. Everyone has a right to health care, although it is a right that we exercise only when we need to – when we become a 'patient'. The nurse, by virtue of her profession, has a duty to enable a patient to exercise that right. The nurse also has a duty to ensure that no harm befalls the patient. There will almost inevitably be occasions when the nurse's rights as an individual will be limited by these two fundamental duties. There may also be occasions when the nurse, in order to fulfil one or both of these duties, will be justified in exercising a personal right to the full. There may be occasions when in order to fulfil her duty to prevent harm to a patient, she would be morally justified in exercising her right to act in accordance with her conscience and not comply with another duty, such as the duty to abide by her contract to her employer. For, as we saw in Chapter 5, one is justified in not acting in accordance with one's duty in order to comply with another, higher duty.

Appeals to conscience

'Childress suggests that an appeal to conscience is based on a desire to preserve one's integrity or wholeness as a person' (Benjamin and Curtis 1981). In making an appeal to conscience one is claiming that to act in a particular way would be a betrayal of one's personal values and beliefs. How one acquires a particular set of values and beliefs is influenced by several factors as we have seen in the early chapters. One's concepts of right and wrong will be influenced by one's family, culture and religion and also by personal experience. Beliefs are personal and subjective. Thus in saying 'I cannot do that because it is against my conscience', one is saying 'It is wrong for *me*; *I* would feel ashamed; *I* would not be true to myself'. When a nurse refuses to carry out a particular procedure on the grounds that it is against her conscience, she is not saying that no nurse should do it. It should be noted that we are here talking about acts which are contrary to an individual's values and beliefs, and not those which could be argued as being contrary to the ethic of the profession.

Generally, it seems, we accept the idea that people have a right to act in accordance with their personal beliefs and values. Henderson (1969) gives as one of her components of basic nursing care: 'Helping the patient practise his religion or conform to his concept of right and wrong.' Henderson's components of nursing care are derived from what she defines as basic human needs. Thus, if to be able to conform to one's concept of right and wrong is a basic human need then nurses too share that need. A *need* is something which is *felt* or *experienced*, and as such something over which an individual has little control. You cannot stop yourself feeling a need. This applies equally to physical needs, such as hunger, to emotional needs, such as the need to be loved, and to spiritual needs, such as the need to worship.

If we accept the idea that nursing is about helping people to meet those needs which they would for themselves if they had the 'necessary strength, will or knowledge', then we have begun to accept the idea that people have a *right* to have those needs met.

The *Universal Declaration of Human Rights* adopted by the United

Nations General Assembly in 1948 proclaims that all people have the right to freedom of thought, conscience and religion and to freedom of opinion and expression. Nurses, no less than any other individuals, possess those rights. Nurses therefore have the right to *appeal to conscience*, to refuse to act in such a way that impinges upon their freedom of belief and expression.

The right to make a conscientious objection is acknowledged by the UKCC Code of Professional Conduct, which states: 'The nurse . . . shall make known to an appropriate person or authority any conscientious objection which may be relevant to professional practice.'

Having established the principle we now consider its application.

Conscientious objection to abortion

Abortion is one procedure to which many nurses hold a conscientious objection. 'Strong and negative attitudes towards patients having elective terminations of pregnancy were expressed by nurses interviewed in a study of gynaecological nurses' attitudes to and opinions of their work' (Webb 1985). Kemp (1984) found that nurses' attitudes to abortion were significantly affected by religious belief.

The 1967 Abortion Act does allow nurses to be excused from participation in abortions if they have a conscientious objection, but not in all cases. In Kemp's study, the majority of nurses surveyed did not realize that, in emergency situations, nurses are required by law to participate in abortion procedures; the 'conscience clause' cannot be invoked. Kemp concludes that there is a need for greater coverage of all aspects of abortion in nurse training.

Given that, (a) the law in the United Kingdom allows nurses to invoke the conscience clause in most cases and (b) the Code requires nurses to make known any conscientious objection they hold, the problem would seem easily solved. A nurse having registered her objection would clearly not choose to work in a situation where abortions were routinely performed. However, the problem is not that simple. Firstly, abortions are frequently carried out, not in separate units or operating theatres, but on a gynaecological ward which provides care for patients with a range of conditions, or within routine gynaecological operating lists. Are nurses who may have a particular interest in gynaecology but who are opposed to abortion to be prevented from pursuing their interest? Secondly, although trained nurses can choose in which specialty they work, nurse learners cannot.

Nurses working on wards or in theatres where abortions form part of the general workload face a dilemma. If they refuse to participate in abortions they may feel that they are placing an additional workload on their colleagues. Their refusal may also cause administrative difficulties about which they may feel uncomfortable. Nurse learners may feel that in refusing to participate in abortions they will miss out on an important part of training. 'Where nurses are ambivalent about abortion, or where they are definitely opposed to it, I think it is extremely important for them to be strong in saying so, and in defending their own moral convictions' (Kenny 1984). In matters of conscience, if one is to be true to oneself, then it may mean going against the general tide and accepting the consequences.

On the issue of abortion, nurses do not fall into two clearly defined camps of those who on the one hand are opposed to it on principle and those on the other hand who have no objection to it. Many nurses would say that abortion is permissible in some circumstances but not others.

For example, Benjamin and Curtis (1981) cite a case in which amniocentesis was to be performed in order to identify the gender of the fetus. The nurse involved had come to believe that abortion was justifiable in cases of a fetus which was extremely likely to be born severely mentally handicapped, although she was in most other circumstances opposed to abortion. In the particular case cited the parents had asked for amniocentesis in order to determine the gender of the child and had made it clear that they intended to request an abortion if the child was male. The doctor involved in the case was prepared to carry out the abortion. The nurse felt the procedure unjustified because she considered that abortion was not justified on these grounds.

The nurse in this situation considered there was a distinction between aborting a perfectly healthy fetus and aborting an unhealthy one. Morally, she had every right to refuse to participate in the procedure on this occasion even though in the past she had willingly consented to participating in abortions.

The nurse as patient's advocate

Where do nurses stand if they feel that patients are being mistreated?

Do nurses have the right to speak out on behalf of patients who perhaps are unable to do so for themselves? These are fundamental questions and ones about which nurses seem very uncertain.

Firstly, though, what do we mean by 'mistreated'? It is obviously a term which can include a range of meanings. It includes the failure on the part of professionals and/or institutions to give adequate care; to allow patients their rights, e.g. to informed consent, to refuse treatment, etc.; the carrying out of unnecessary treatment; and it also includes physical and mental abuse.

The International Code of Nursing Ethics (1973) states: 'The fundamental responsibility of a nurse is to promote health, prevent illness, restore health and alleviate suffering . . . . The nurse takes appropriate action to safeguard the individual when his care is endangered by a co-worker or any other person.'

The nurse then has not merely the *right* but a *responsibility* to act on behalf of the patient if she feels that he is being mistreated. However, as several reports in the press and elsewhere have shown, it is not always easy for nurses to take on the role of patient's advocate (Beardshaw 1981).

The Report of a Committee of Enquiry investigating allegations concerning the care and treatment of patients at Saint Augustine's Hospital, Canterbury in 1976 concluded that a degree of force which exceeded legitimate persuasion had been used to administer electro-convulsive therapy (ECT) to unwilling informal patients on many occasions (Beardshaw 1981). If a nurse believes that any treatment is being incorrectly or unnecessarily carried out then she has (a) a *right* to refuse to participate and (b) a *duty* to make a complaint.

The refusal to participate can be made on the basis that the patient's rights are being undermined or by making an appeal to conscience. If the nurse has reason for believing that, as the Enquiry cited above found, the treatment is being administered against the patient's wishes and that the patient is being coerced into giving consent, then she has a right to refuse to participate. The question of ECT is a very controversial one; its therapeutic value has been questioned (Fromer 1981). If the therapy used to change or control behaviour involves the infliction of pain or a loss of dignity, then it is even more questionable.

It would seem then that a nurse could, and should be able to, refuse to participate in a form of therapy, such as ECT, on the grounds that it is against her conscience.

The refusal by a nurse to participate in certain procedures in general, or in individual cases, is not the end of the matter. The procedure will still in all probability be carried out. The question then is whether the nurse has a right to take it further. As has already been seen it can be difficult enough for a nurse to refuse to participate in certain procedures. It can be even more difficult for the nurse to take on the role of patient's advocate. Beardshaw found that nurses working in mental hospitals frequently did not make complaints about ill-treatment of patients for several reasons. The main reasons for remaining silent were fear of victimization, fear of cover-ups, and that complaints would achieve nothing.

If, and there seems little doubt that it is so, nurses have a right, indeed a duty, to speak out on behalf of their patients, then the profession, employers and society as a whole have a duty to allow them freedom to exercise that right. There are formal procedures available to nurses to make complaints, but, as Beardshaw discovered, these can be very formidible. Furthermore, nurses are not always aware of their rights or the avenues available to them. If they do initiate a complaint they may not always follow it through if they meet with difficulties and obstructions. 'Staying the course may call for great reserves of stamina and determination particularly if the issues are multiple' (Thorold 1981).

Suppose that a nurse has evidence of maltreatment of a patient who is unable to take any action himself. Her first move would be to make a complaint through the management hierarchy to her employing authority. If she feels that the complaint is not dealt with satisfactorily, that no action is taken or the matter is 'hushed up', what further steps can she take? There are several other channels open to her. She can raise the matter with her professional association or Trade Union; she can, in the United Kingdom, report it to the Health Service Commissioner; seek the help of the local Community Health Council; or report it to the UKCC. Unfortunately in pursuing these avenues she may be made to feel that she is being disloyal to her colleagues or employer. However, these various bodies exist in order to protect the nurse, the patient or both, and nurses have a right, moral and legal, to avail themselves of them.

Complaints officially lodged in any of the ways mentioned may result in a formal enquiry being set up, either an internal enquiry on the part of the Health Authority or a Government Enquiry. The findings of such enquiries may or may not be made public. The concern is that if enquiry findings are not publicized then little or no action may result. Furthermore, nurses may fear that if findings are published then their hospital will be brought into disrepute, which would reflect upon their own and their colleagues' professional reputations.

The next question is 'Do nurses have the right to draw public attention to cases of malpractice?' 'It is curious, given the value that is supposed to be placed on freedom of speech and freedom of the press in Britain, that so many legal doubts remain about the right of an employee to give information to the press' (Beardshaw 1981). As far as the law stands, at least in the way in which it operates in practice, going to the press is a last resort which should only be undertaken if all other official avenues have been exhausted. The nurse who goes to the press is likely to be sanctioned by the law.[1]

From a purely moral standpoint one could argue that it is in the public interest that information should be made known. The public have a right to know what is going on. Members of the public have a right to know how safe they will be if they submit themselves to the care of the Health Service. The nurse may therefore find herself in a position where her moral convictions conflict with her legal rights and duties. We shall return to this vexed question of morality versus legality later, but first we consider one further issue.

Withdrawal of labour

Do nurses have a right to withdraw their labour and would they ever be justified in going on strike? First, let us consider the question as to whether there is a *right to strike*. If such a right exists then it is a *welfare* right and not a *natural* or *option* right. That is to say that the right to strike cannot be equated with such rights as those to life or to freedom.

The argument that one has a right to strike can be made on the basis of a fundamental right to justice. The right to justice means that one has a right to fair terms of employment, a right to adequate working conditions and to reasonable reward. If one is denied these rights then one has a right to strike in order to obtain them. As far as nurses and other health workers are concerned, however, other fundamental rights have to be taken into account. The patient, indeed the population as a whole, has a right to health care. Inevitably if nurses exert a right to strike they will restrict the rights of others to health care. Rights cannot be rights if they are exercised at the price of harm to others.

Any industrial action in the Health Service, be it an all-out strike, a work-to-rule or a refusal to deal with nothing other than 'emergencies', will harm patients. It will mean increased waiting time for treatment, delay in diagnosis and a deterioration in standards of care. Patients will therefore suffer. To strike or take any form of industrial action for the purposes of improving pay is morally unjustifiable. Would it though be justifiable in order to improve health care or to prevent harm to patients?

Some have claimed that nurses would be justified in taking industrial action in order to draw attention to, and hopefully rectify, inadequate health care provision. Utilitarians would argue that to strike in order to achieve the end of improved health care was justified, on the grounds that, while some individuals might suffer, the end aimed for was the greater good for the greater number. The argument against this contention is that while nurses as a whole have a duty toward the population as a whole they also have individual duties and responsibilities toward individual patients. The nurse's duty towards the individual patient already under her care supersedes the collective duty of all nurses toward the whole population.

If on the other hand nurses were ordered by their employer or the government to act in a way which was clearly harmful to patients then they could be justified in refusing so to do. 'If, for example, under a Nazi Government a policy decision was taken to perform selective euthanasia on demented elderly patients, one would hope nurses would be prepared to strike rather than implement the policy' (Thompson et al 1983). In less dramatic situations nurses would have to decide whether patients would suffer more because of poor conditions, lack of manpower or resources, or as a result of industrial action.

Another possible justification for withdrawal of labour might be if nurses were required to work in conditions which were harmful to themselves. If, for example, a Health Authority failed to provide nursing staff with the correct protective clothing or equipment for caring for patients with a highly contagious disease, would the nurses be justified in refusing to care for those patients? Here the nurses would have to balance the risk to their own health against the risks to the patients. Clearly the onus is on the Health Authority, indeed on society as a whole, to provide nurses with safe working conditions and the tools to do the job it requires of them. Society does not have the right to expect that nurses should put their own health or lives at risk in order to fulfil their duty to society. In such a situation the decision has to be one for each individual nurse and those who refuse to work under such circumstances should not be condemned.

Morality versus legality

'Most stable societies have a long tradition of law and custom that embodies the established moral consensus of that society' (Thompson et al 1983). Thus in many cases what is right or wrong in law may also be right or wrong morally. However, certain acts may be morally, but not legally, wrong, and vice versa. For example, in the United Kingdom, to take one's own life is not illegal, but many would claim that it is morally wrong. The law does not give a moral sanction to act in a particular way.

Again one might claim that a law is in itself immoral and that one would therefore be morally justified in breaking that law. Throughout history there have been numerous examples of laws which people have felt morally justified in violating. It is the stuff of which martyrs are made. Even in modern times there have been, and are, many examples. Martin Luther King and his followers felt morally justified in violating the law to protest against the immoral race laws in the United States. Apartheid is considered by many to be morally wrong and therefore, it is claimed, people are morally justified in violating the South African laws of apartheid. The argument of some members of Peace Movements is that possession of nuclear weapons is in itself immoral and that one is justified in protesting against their possession even if doing so means violating the law of the land.

Within the context of health care it is easy to envisage extreme circumstances, such as the example of euthanasia under a Nazi Government referred to earlier, in which nurses and other health professionals would be morally justified in breaking or refusing to obey the law. Generally speaking, nurses do not find themselves faced with such clear-cut situations. In Chapter 8 it was suggested that compliance with the order of a Court of Law to divulge information about a patient was morally justified. One could, on the other hand, argue that a nurse would be morally justified, and in some cases have a moral duty, to disobey the court's order and face the legal consequences. In the case of contractual law, a nurse would be morally justified in not fulfilling her duty to her employer in order to comply with the higher duty to care for her patient. Again she might be found guilty in law and have to pay the consequences of such action. Moral rights or obligations might *excuse* one from obeying the law, but they do not *suspend* the law.

'There will always be acts that are morally permissible or obligatory, but not legal, and vice versa' (Benjamin and Curtis 1981). The reasons are basically two-fold, firstly, because the nature of ethical enquiry is such that changing circumstances are constantly causing people to re-evaluate and re-interpret moral values, and secondly because it is impossible to legislate to cover every conceivable situation without imposing unacceptable limitations on personal freedom and privacy. Therefore, while one can argue a strong case that in a reasonably just society one has a prima facie obligation to obey the law, that obligation can be overridden in order to comply with a higher, more stringent moral obligation.

Codes of ethics – values and limitations

Benjamin and Curtis (1981) contend that codes of professional ethics contain two categories of statements – *statements of creed* and *commandments*. Statements of *creed* or *belief* 'affirm professional regard for high ideals of conduct and personally commit members of the profession to honour them, thus constituting a sort of oath of professional conduct' (Benjamin and Curtis 1981). An example of such statements is to be found in both the International Council of Nurses Code (1973) and that of the American Nurses' Association (1976). 'The fundamental responsibility of the nurse is fourfold; to promote health, to prevent illness, to restore health and to alleviate suffering.' Such statements provide a valuable reminder of the special responsibilities placed on nurses. All patients are to a greater or lesser degree vulnerable and dependent on the professionals' decisions. Patients and the public in general need to be assured that they will not be exploited nor placed at risk when submitting to the care of nurses. Codes of ethics can serve to give them that assurance. 'Each registered nurse, midwife and health visitor shall act, at all times, in such a manner as to justify public trust and confidence, to uphold and enhance the good standing of the profession, to serve the interests of society, and above all to safeguard the interests of individual patients and clients' (UKCC 1984).

Professional codes also contain *commandments*. The purpose of these is two-fold. Firstly, they provide an enforceable standard of minimally decent conduct that allows the profession to discipline its members. For example, 'The registered nurse, midwife or health visitor shall avoid any abuse of the privileged relationship which exists with patients/clients and of the privileged access allowed to their property, residence or workplace' (UKCC 1984). Without such published and acknowledged statements the UKCC and equivalent bodies in other countries, would clearly have difficulty in making decisions about admitting people to, or striking them from, the professional register. Secondly, such statements indicate in general terms some of the ethical considerations professionals must take into account when deciding conduct. For example, the nurse shall 'take every reasonable opportunity to maintain and improve professional knowledge and competence' (UKCC 1984).

Professional codes thus serve three main functions. They serve to reassure the public, they provide guidelines for the profession to discipline and regulate its members, and they provide a framework on which individual members can formulate decisions. They do, however, inevitably have their limitations.

Codes of ethics cannot and do not provide answers to each and every situation. Clearly if the intention is that all nurses should read them then codes of ethics have to be brief and comprehensible. They have also to be *acceptable* to all nurses. There is then the danger that they will become vague, abstract and so general that they cannot, without significant interpretation, be applied to many specific situations.

On the other hand, if they attempt to be very specific and comprehensive they are likely not to be acceptable to all and will become extremely lengthy and unlikely as a consequence to be read fully by many nurses. It is in any case impossible to write a code of ethics which will provide precise answers for any and every situation. However detailed the code of ethics there comes a point when the individual has to make a decision for her/himself.

Conclusion – making ethical decisions

Ethical decisions, like other professional decisions, should be informed. Many of the ethical issues in nursing and health care are emotive. Most of us approach such issues as abortion, euthanasia, and apportioning health funds with strongly felt emotions. The first step in ethical decision making is to avoid making a purely emotional response.

How then should one approach ethical decisions? Firstly, one needs a framework to guide one's thinking. Professional codes of ethics are one aid. A knowledge and understanding of ethical theories is also necessary, not only to provide one with a framework on which to work but also to give one an understanding of how others might approach the subject. The purpose of books such as this one is to enhance knowledge and understanding of ethical theories. Secondly, it is important to be able to argue from a sound knowledge base. This means having a grounding in such areas as the biological and social sciences, the nature and treatment of diseases, and keeping abreast of developments in nursing and nursing research. It also means gathering all the relevant facts pertaining to the specific situation. Thirdly, one needs to be able to argue one's case clearly and logically and avoid leaping to conclusions on the basis of too little or inaccurate information.

No one can withdraw from moral decision making and nurses, along with members of other professions, because of the nature of their work are faced with making decisions of a moral or ethical nature more frequently than other members of society. The importance for nurses of examining their own beliefs and values and of understanding how they arrived at them cannot be overemphasized. Nor can it be overemphasized that nurses should not seek to impose their own values on either their colleagues or patients. By the same token no one should allow themselves to be easily swayed by emotive arguments. Perhaps the overriding principle in moral decision making is *honesty* – honesty toward others but more importantly honesty with and to oneself. 'To thine own self be true' (*Hamlet*).

Notes

1 For further discussion of this issue see Thorold, O. (1981), 'Nurse Whistleblowers and the Law'. In Beardshaw, V. (1981), *Conscientious Objectors at Work*, London: Social Audit.

References

Beardshaw, V. (1981), *Conscientious Objectors at Work*, London: Social Audit.
Fromer, M.J. (1981), *Ethical Issues in Health Care*, St. Louis: C.V. Mosby.
Henderson, V. (1969), *Basic Principles of Nursing Care*, Geneva: ICN.
International Council of Nurses (1973), *Code for Nurses*, Geneva: ICN.

Kemp, J. (1984), Attitudes to Abortion, *Nursing Mirror*, April 25, Vol. 158, No. 17, pp. 34–35.

Kenny, M. (1984), All in the Line of Duty?, *Nursing Mirror*, May 16, Vol. 158, No. 20, pp. 22–23.

Thompson, I.E., Melia, K.M. and Boyd, K.M. (1983), *Nursing Ethics*, Edinburgh: Churchill Livingstone.

Thorold, O. (1981), 'Nurse Whistleblowers and the Law'. In Beardshaw, V. (1981), *Conscientious Objectors at Work*, London: Social Audit.

UKCC (United Kingdom Central Council for Nursing, Midwifery and Health Visiting) (1984), *Code of Professional Conduct for the Nurse, Midwife and Health Visitor*, 2nd Edition, London: UKCC.

Webb, C. (1985), Nurses' Attitudes to Therapeutic Abortion, *Nursing Times*, January 2, Vol. 81, No. 1, pp. 44–47. 1985.

Further reading

On appeals to conscience

Benjamin, M. and Curtis, J. (1981), *Ethics in Nursing*, New York: Oxford University Press. See references to 'Conscience' and 'Conscientious Refusal'.

Thompson, I.E., Melia, K.M. and Boyd, K.M. (1983), *Nursing Ethics*, Edinburgh: Churchill Livingstone. See Chapter 3, 'Responsibility and Accountability in Nursing'.

On withdrawal of labour

Benjamin, M. and Curtis, J. (1981), *Ethics in Nursing*, New York: Oxford University Press. See references to 'Strikes'.

Thompson, I.E., Melia, K.M. and Boyd, K.M. (1983), *Nursing Ethics*, Edinburgh: Churchill Livingstone. See Chapter 6, 'Nurses and Society' for a full discussion of this topic.

On morality versus legality

Edwards, P. (ed) (1967), *Encyclopedia of Philosophy*, New York: Macmillan and Free Press. See 'Responsibility, Moral and Legal', Arnold S. Kaufman.

Reich, W.J. (1978), *The Encyclopedia of Bioethics*, New York: Macmillan and Free Press. See 'Law and Morality', Brody, B.A.

Smith, J.P. (1983), The Relationship between Rights and Responsibilities in Health Care: A Dilemma for Nurses, *Journal of Advanced Nursing*, Vol. 8, pp. 437–440.

Thompson, I.E., Melia, K.M. and Boyd, K.M. (1983), *Nursing Ethics*, Edinburgh: Churchill Livingstone. See Chapter 2, section 4 on 'Ethics, Law and Religion'.

On codes of ethics

Benjamin, M. and Curtis, J. (1981), *Ethics in Nursing*, New York: Oxford University Press. See references to 'Codes'.

Veatch, R.M. (1981), *A Theory of Medical Ethics*, New York: Basic Books Inc. See Chapter 4, 'The Problems with Professional Physician Ethics'.

INDEX

Abortion
    Catholic teaching on, 17–18, 73, 85
    conscientious objection to, 1, 141–2
    ethical debate on, 1, 5, 74–9, 84, 142
    eugenic, 77–8
    therapeutic, 75–6
Abortion Act 1967, 75–6, 141
Act utilitarianism, 43–4
Acute services, relative importance of, 32–3
Agape (love), theological theme, 20
Ahimsa, Hindu notion of, 22–3
Altruism, component of ethical codes, 37, 39
American Hospital Association (1972), Patients' Bill of Rights, 104, 113, 135
American Nurses' Association (ANA) Code for Nurses (1976)
    categories of statements in, 148
    on confidentiality, 102
    on nurses' responsibility and duty, 58, 123, 135
Amniocentesis, technique for determining
    abnormal embryo, 78
    gender of embryo, 142
Apartheid laws, justification for disobeying, 147
Aquinas, Thomas, on natural law, 17, 20
Aristotle, on rational pleasures, 38
Arristupus, on hedonism, 37–8
Authoritarianism, 37

Autonomy
    nurses', 122, 131–3, 137
    patients' 88–90, 99

Beardsaw, V., on maltreatment of patients, 143–5
Beauchamp, T.L., on confidential information, 105
Belief, see Creed
Benjamin, M.
    on appeals to conscience, 140, 142
    on codes of nursing ethics, 57, 148
    on nurses' duty to patients, 124
Bentham, Jeremy, on utilitarianism, 11, 42–3
Birth control, see Contraception
Brown, Louise, birth following IVF, 79

Campbell, A.V., on abortion, 74–5
Caraka Samhita, the, 22
Cardoza, B.N., on patients' consent, 94
Catholicism
    medical ethics, 13, 17–19, 25, 35, 73, 85
    on sanctity of life, 17–18, 27
    see also Christianity
Child (children)
    handicapped, 20–1, 24–5, 30, 66, 77–8
    informed consent to treatment for, 96, 113–14
    unborn, see Embryo(s)
Childress, J.F., on confidential information, 105

153

Christianity
  ethical literature, 13–14, 19, 67
  teaching on
    euthanasia, 67
    natural law, 7
    respect for the dead, 16
    sanctity of life, 14, 24–5, 67
    sexuality, 18
  see also Catholicism, Judaeo-
        Christian tradition *and*
        Protestantism
Codes of ethics
  categories of statements
      contained in, 148–9
  values and limitations, 148–9
  see also specific Codes, e.g.
      American Nurses'
      Association (ANA) Code
      for Nurses (1976)
Cold Research Unit, volunteers
    for experimentation at,
    90–1
Commandments, in codes of
    professional ethics, 57,
    148–9
Communist medical ethics, 23–
    4, 48
Complaints procedures,
    maltreatment of patients,
    144–5
Confidentiality (of information)
  assessment of, 101–10
  in nurse–patient relationship,
    101–10, 147–8
Conscientious objection, 140–2
  to abortion, 1, 141–2
Consent (from relatives), to
    treatment, 96–7, 113–14
Consent (patients')
  to experimentation, 93–4
  to treatment
    educated, 95
    informed, 94–9, 111, 143
Contraception
  Catholic teaching on, 17–20

Muslim teaching on, 21–2
  natural law on, 9–10
Corpse(s)
  anatomical dissection, 21
  postmortems, 16
  see also Death *and* Organ
    transplants
Covenant, theological theme, 19–
    20
Creed, statements of, in codes of
    professional ethics, 57, 148
Curtis, J.
  on appeals to conscience, 140,
    142
  on codes of nursing ethics, 57,
    148
  on nurses' duty to patients, 124

Dead body(-ies), *see* Corpse(s)
Death
  right to, 65, 68
  see also Corpse(s), Euthanasia,
    Killing, Life *and*
    Terminally ill patients
Decision making, ethical, *see*
    Ethical decision making
Demy, N.J., on informed consent,
    95
Deontological (duty-based)
    theories governing human
    behaviour, 48–51, 59
Disabled, *see* Mentally
    handicapped *and* Physically
    handicapped
Dock, S., on nurse's obedience to
    doctors, 122
Doctor–nurse relationship, *see*
    Nurse–doctor relationship
Doctor–patient relationship
  covenant, 20
  euthanasia and, 69–70
  paternalism in, 40, 115
  truth telling in, 112–14
Double effect, principle of, 5–7
  Catholicism and, 19

situations, decision-making
    criteria, 6–7
Down's syndrome, children
        suffering from
    due to genetic defects, 77
    quality of life of, 30, 66
Duty
    concept of, 1, 48
    nurse's, to patients, 51, 143
    theories governing human
        behaviour based on, 48–
        51, 59

Electroconvulsive therapy (ECT),
    controversial use of, 143
Embryo(s)
    as result of IVF, 79–80
    experimentation on, 83–4
    identification of abnormal, 78
    stages of development, 72–3
    start of human life in, 29, 72–5,
        80
    transfer, 79–80, 81–2, 84
    see also Abortion
End-justifies-the-means ethic, 1–5,
    11, 50
    applied to euthanasia, 2, 64
    implications of, 2–3
    see also Utilitarianism
Epicurus, on moderation of sensual
    pleasure, 38
Ethical decision making
    criteria for, 6–7
    cultural influences on, 13–23
    independent, for nurses, 123–4
    informed approach to, 149–50
    natural law guidelines, 8–9, 11
    patients' involvement in, 87
    quality of life considerations, 30–
        3, 35
    terminally ill patients, 6–7, 70,
        115–16
    utilitarian considerations, 45
Eugenic abortion, 77–8
Euthanasia

active, 62–3
Catholic teaching on, 17–18
defined, 61–2
ethical debate on, 1–2, 5, 33,
    62–9
Hindu teaching on, 22
Jewish teaching on, 15
on demand, 69–70
passive, 62–3
problems of administration, 69–
    70
voluntary, 64–5, 69–70
Experimentation
    on embryos, 83–4
    on mentally handicapped, 33, 96–8
    on Nazi concentration camp
        inmates, 2, 4–5, 28, 90
    on patients, 1, 90–4, 97–8, 126
    therapeutic and non-
        therapeutic, 91–2

Fetus, *see* Embryo(s)
Firth, Roderick, on natural law, 8
Fletcher, J.F.
    on agape (love), 20
    on euthanasia, 62–3, 65, 68
Fromer, M.J.
    on IVF, 79–80
    on option and welfare rights, 51–
        3, 55
    on patients' rights, 97, 99, 143
    on sanctity of life, 27, 35

Geriatric patients, quality of life,
    30–2
Gesisah (state of), Jewish notion of,
    15, 22
Goal-based (teleological) theories
    governing human
    behaviour, 37–47, 48–9
Golding, M.P., on option rights,
    52–3
Good and bad (evil)
    concepts of, 1
    consequences of actions, 4–5

Gray, Dr Hugh, on euthanasia, 64–5

Handicapped, *see* Mentally handicapped *and* Physically handicapped
Happiness, human, utilitarianism and, 4–5, 11, 42–6, 76
Hargreaves, I., on autonomy of nurse, 131
Health care, right to, 51, 55–6, 139, 145
Hedonism, 37–8
Henderson, Virginia, on components of basic nursing care, 1, 31, 140
Hersley, Gerald, on paternalism, 40
Hinduism
    medical ethics, 13, 22–3, 25
    on sanctity of life, 28–9
Hippocratic tradition, 14, 64, 95
Human life
    constituents of, 29–30
    distinguished from other forms, 28–30
    start of (in embryo), 29, 72–5, 80
    see also Death, Life, Quality of life *and* Sanctity of life
Human rights
    defined, 51
    United Nations Declaration, 7, 51, 68, 140–1

In vitro fertilization (IVF)
    ethical debate on, 79–80, 84
    mechanics of, 79
Incest, termination of pregnancy following, 77
Individual, needs and rights of the, 32, 39–42, 46
Infertility, problems and solutions, 81–2
Information
    confidential, 101–10, 147–8

patients' rights to, 55, 87, 112–13
    terminally ill patients, 113–20
    see also Informed consent *and* Truth telling
Informed consent
    patients', 94–9, 111, 143
    relatives', 96–7, 113–14
International Council of Nurses (ICN) Code (1973)
    on categories of statements, 57, 148
    on confidentiality, 102
    on nurses' duty and responsibility, 135, 143
Intuition, natural law determined by, 8–9
Inviolability of human life
    concept of, 17, 27–8, 30
    see also Sanctity of life
Islam
    laws, 22
    medical ethics, 13, 21–2, 25

Jacobovits, I., on Jewish medical ethics, 14
Judaeo–Christian tradition
    biblical ethical code, 13–14, 67
    medical ethics, 13–14
    teaching on sanctity of life, 14–16, 27, 67
    see also Judaism *and* Christianity
Judaism
    ethical literature, 13–14, 67
    laws, 15–16
    medical ethics, 14–16, 25, 48
    teaching on
        revelation, 7
        sanctity of life, 14–15, 67

Kant, Immanuel
    on duty, 50–1
    on lying, 112
    on respect for persons, 28
    on universal law of nature, 8, 11–12

Kemp, on conscientious objection
    to abortion, 141
Killing
    ethical debate on, 2, 18, 20–5
    see also Abortion, Death *and*
        Euthanasia
King, Martin Luther, protest
    against race laws, 147

Laws, immoral, justification for
    disobeying, 110, 145, 147–8
Life
    Hindu respect for, 28–9
    human, *see* Human life
    right to, 17–18, 68, 79
    see also Death, Quality of life *and*
        Sanctity of life
Love (agape), theological theme,
    20
Lying
    ethics of, 3–4, 112
    see also Truth telling

Majority
    needs and rights of the, 42–5
    see also Utilitarianism
Maltreatment of patients
    complaints procedures, 144–5
    nurses' reaction to, 143–5
Marxism
    medical ethics, 13, 23–4, 48
    role of the State, 23–4, 45–6
Mentally handicapped, the
    attitudes of various belief
        systems to, 20–2, 24–5,
        29–30
    children, 20–1, 24–5, 30, 66, 77–
        8
    consent to treatment, 96–7, 113–
        14
    experiments on, 33, 96–8
    quality of life of, 30, 32–3, 66, 78
    sterilization of, 97
    vulnerability of, 57
Mercy killing, *see* Euthanasia

Mill, John Stuart, on
    utilitarianism, 11, 43
Muslim, *see* Islam

Natural (moral) law
    Catholic teaching based on, 17
    determining, 7–9
    ethical decision making based
        on, 8–9, 11
    principles derived from, 17–19
Nazi experiments on
    concentration camp inmates, 2,
        4–5, 28, 90
    Jews, 33
    mentally handicapped, 33, 96
Nelson, J.B., on passive
    euthanasia, 62
New-born child (mentally or
        physically handicapped)
    ethical considerations, 20–1, 24–
        5, 77–8
    quality of life of, 30, 66, 78
Nurse–doctor relationship
    conflicts arising from
        autonomy of nurse, 122, 131–
            3, 137
        changing role of nurse, 127–31
        clinical judgement, 124–7
        divided loyalties, 133
        professional loyalty, 134–6
    paternalism in, 40, 115
    role of obedience in, 122–4, 127,
        136
    truth telling in, 122–3
Nurse–patient relationship
    confidentiality in, 101–10, 147–8
    elements of, 101
    euthanasia and, 69
    paternalism in, 40
    truth telling in, 112–14
Nurses' rights, 139–50
    see also specific rights. e.g. Strike,
        right to
Nursing Process
    assessment of patients' needs,
        120

philosophy, 40–1, 120, 131–2

Obedience, traditional attribute of
    nurses, 122–4, 127, 136
Observation, natural law
    determined by, 8–9
Oken, D., on informing terminal
    patients, 115
Option rights, 52–3, 139, 145
Organ transplants
    Jewish attitude to, 16
    Muslim attitude to, 21
    relative value of, 32
Ovum
    donation, 82
    in vitro fertilization of, 79–80

Paternalism, 40, 99, 115
Patients
    autonomy and dignity of, 88–90,
        99
    avoidance of harm to, 87–99, 139
    experimentation on, 1, 90–4, 97–
        8, 126
    maltreatment of, 143, 5
    see also Doctor–patient
        relationship, Nurse–
        patient relationship *and*
        Terminally ill patients
Patients' rights, 40–1, 79, 143
    American Hospital Association
        Bill of Rights, 104, 113,
        135
    movement, 15, 41
    see also Information, Informed
        consent *and specific rights*,
        e.g. Health care, right to
Peace Movements, 147
Physically handicapped, the
    attitudes of various belief
        systems to, 20–2, 24–5,
        29–30
    children, 21, 24–5, 30, 77–8
    quality of life of, 30, 66
    vulnerability of, 57

Placebos, ethics of administering,
    126–7
Privacy, right to, 79
Procreation
    sexuality and, 18–19
    see also Contraception
Professionalization of nursing,
    123–4
Protestantism
    medical ethics, 13, 19–20, 25
    see also Christianity

Quality of life
    decision making based on, 31–3,
        35, 66
    expounded, 30–3
    in old age, 30–2
    of mentally handicapped, 30,
        32–3, 66, 78
    versus sanctity of life, 34–5, 66
    see also Sanctity of life
Quinlan, Karen, right to die, 65

Rape, termination of pregnancy
    following, 77
Rayner, K., on euthanasia, 67, 69
Reason, human, natural law
    determined by, 7–9, 17
Refusal to participate in treatment,
    nurse's right, 142–4
Refuse treatment, patient's right
    to, 56, 97–9, 143
Reincarnation, doctrine of, 22
Relatives
    information, terminally ill
        patients, 114
    informed consent from, 96, 113–
        14
Responsibility
    concept of, 48
    nurses', 57–9, 143
Revelation, natural law determined
    by, 7–9
Right and wrong, concepts of, 1–
    11, 140

Right to, *see specific right, e.g.* Health care, right to
Rights
 concept of, 48–9
 see also specific rights, e.g. Patients' rights
 Rights-based theories governing human behaviour, 49, 51–6, 59
 implications of, 53–6
Roper, Nancy, on twelve activities of daily living, 31
Royal College of Nursing (RCN) Code of Professional Conduct (1976), 48, 57, 90
Rule utilitarianism, 43–4

Sacredness of life
 concept of, 17, 27–8
 see also Sanctity of life
Saint Augustine's Hospital, Canterbury, investigation into maltreatment of patients, 143
Sanctity of life
 expounded, 27–30
 religious belief in, 14–16, 22, 24–5, 27, 67
 versus quality of life, 34–5, 66
 see also Quality of life
Sartre, Jean Paul, on quality of life in old age, 31
Self-interest, human behaviour motivated by, 37–9
Sexuality
 Catholic attitude to, 18–19
 Jewish attitude to, 15–16
 Muslim attitude to, 22
 natural law applied to, 9–10
Slave trade (African), ethics of, 33
Sollito, S., on human experimentation, 91
State, role of, in Communist society, 23–4, 45–6

Steptoe, Dr Patrick, on birth of Louise Brown, 82
Sterilization
 Catholic teaching on, 19
 of mentally handicapped females, 97
Stewardship, principle of, 17
Strike, right to, 145–7
Suicide
 Catholic teaching on, 18
 voluntary euthanasia, 64–5, 69–70
Surrogate motherhood, 80–2

Teleological (goal-based) theories governing human behaviour, 37–47, 48–9
Terminally ill patients
 information for, 113–20
 decision problems, 6–7, 70, 115–16
 identifying responsibility for, 177–19
 rights, 55
Thompson, I.E.
 on morality versus legality, 147
 on nurse–doctor relationship, 133
 on nurses' right to strike, 146
Thorold, O., on nurses' complaints of maltreatment of patients, 144
Totality, principle of, 18
Treatment
 consent to
  patients', 94–9, 111, 143
  relatives', 96–7, 113–14
 extraordinary means, 35
 refusal
  nurses', 142–4
  patients', 56, 97–9, 143
Trowell, Hugh, on euthanasia, 70
Truth telling
 defined, 111–12
 ethics of, 3–5, 112–13

in doctor–patient relationship, 112–14
in nurse–doctor relationship, 122–3
to terminal patients, 113–20
see also Information *and* Lying

UKCC Code of Professional Conduct (1984)
categories of statements in, 148–9
on confidentiality, 102 ✳
on conscientious objection, 141
on nurse–doctor relationship, 118, 135
on nurses' responsibility, 58
Unborn child, *see* Embryo(s)
Unconscious patient, relatives' consent to treatment for, 96
United Nations' *Declaration of Human Rights*, 7, 51, 68, 140–1
Universal benefit, behaviour motivated to promote, 45–6
University of Rochester Medical Centre, survey on informing terminal patients, 115
Utilitarianism
applied to abortion, 76
human happiness and, 4–5, 11, 42–6, 76
nurses' right to strike, 146
see also End-justifies-the-means ethic

Varga, A.C.
on abortion, 74, 76–8
on experimentation
embryos, 83
patients, 90
on IVF, 80, 82
on information to terminal patients, 113–15
on useless and useful means of treatment, 35
Veatch, R.M.
on human experimentation, 91
on informing patients, 95, 112–13
on principle of double effect, 19

Webb, C., on conscientious objection to abortion, 141
Weber, L.J., on euthanasia, 65–8
Welfare rights, 52–3, 139, 145
Withdrawal of labour
justification of, 146–7
nurses' rights, 145–7
Women
right to abortion, 79
sterilization of mentally handicapped, 97
World Medical Assembly, Declaration of Helsinki (guidelines for human experimentation), 91, 94